Behavioral Covenants in Congregations

A HANDBOOK FOR HONORING DIFFERENCES

GILBERT R. RENDLE

An Alban Institute Publication

Library of Congress Card Number 98-73677

ISBN 1-56699-209-5

for Lynne

CONTENTS

INTRODUCTION

This book is about a common problem in North American Protestant, Catholic, and Jewish congregations. Many of our congregations are plagued with uncivil behavior. Some experience it daily. For others it simmers beneath a polite surface waiting to break through with the slightest provocation. Where one would hope to find dialogue, there is instead competitive debate. Where one would hope to see an honest owning of feelings, there are instead anonymous communications. Where one would hope that leaders would deal with clear opinions and facts, there is instead rumor and hearsay.

The fact is that many local congregations, which once spoke openly about themselves as "family" and now casually refer to themselves as communities, are likely to exhibit behavior that is a poor example of either family or community. My work as a senior consultant with the Alban Institute regularly puts me into working relationships with congregations that are experiencing conflict and in which members exhibit behaviors which stand in contrast to my understanding of the teachings of their faith. I have witnessed small groups in which some members demand that other members leave the room because they do not trust speaking in front of them. I have interviewed congregational members who have leveled accusations against others based not on what they themselves have experienced or witnessed but rather on hearsay information repeated and embellished by friends whose personal preferences were not being met. I have worked with a congregation in which very wealthy and powerful members of the governing board held a formal victory party in the home of one of the leaders to celebrate their success in forcing their rector not only out of the church but out of town as well. He was sufficiently hurt and damaged that he would tell no one, not even his bishop, where he had gone. I have counseled with clergy who have considered or chosen to take legal action against their governing boards, casting all blame on the board rather than accepting their part in a difficult relationship that would require change and the seeking of forgiveness in order to be productive in ministry.

It is very common for our Alban Institute senior consultants to be asked to work with a congregation to help them "deal with their diversity." The request often comes with much pain and discomfort as the people in the congregation admit to the difficulties they have had in getting along with one another. Yet, when we as consultants look at the group that we are working with, we see more marks of sameness than of difference, more homogeneity than heterogeneity. Often we work with groups that are largely, if not exclusively, of one race and who appear to share similar lifestyles and daily behaviors. I found it ironic that when I worked with one very seriously divided congregation, I found that the large majority of members who attended the meetings wore casual, outdoor clothing obviously purchased through the same mail order catalog. Not only were these people similar in many ways, but they even dressed alike! Nonetheless I had been called to help them work through the differences that divided them and through the callous, damaging behavior that they had experienced at one another's hands because of those differences.

Although my relationship as a consultant makes me privy to more extreme examples of uncivil behavior than others who live and work in congregations, all clergy and laity commonly encounter behaviors that fall short of faith standards. I suggest that such behaviors are rooted, in part, in an inheritance based in cultural and congregational assumptions that we are now beginning to understand. Chief among those assumptions is the current notion that as individuals we do not have to defer to the need of the larger group, be it family, congregation, or community.

It is also important to note at the very beginning of this book that the differences which disrupt and divide many of our congregations can range from controversial issues (such as the ordination of gays) to subtle differences (such as who will organize the spring clean-up crew). Many of our congregations have learned to accommodate themselves to the more obvious differences and controversial moral questions regarding the highly visible divisions of race, gender, and age that marked the 1960s, 1970s, and 1980s.

What is more often at the heart of the disruption of many congregations today, however, are differences that are more subtle and hidden.
Because they are subtle and hidden, we have never formulated a common language to talk openly about them. For example, even what appear
to be large issues, such as homosexuality, public prayer, and abortion,
rest on much more subtle differences and assumptions about the source
of authority in our lives. Does authority come from an understanding of
Scripture as the singular, clear, and definitive authority for making
judgments about right and wrong? Or does authority come from an understanding of our experience that is based on our scriptural foundation
but continues to be shaped and informed in further revelations from
social and physical sciences and from common practice in daily life?
To people in many of our congregations who come with less than clear
understandings of their own spiritual heritage and with a diminished
understanding of the theology and polity of their denomination, such
differences of understanding scriptural authority seem much too subtle.
There is no common language with which to converse.

If larger national and global issues have such subtle underpinnings,
imagine the subtlety of the differences that can be found in our generational subgroups in congregations. For example, it is common for longer-
tenured members to have learned the lessons of tradition and to respect
the formality of worship that remains relatively unchanged from week to
week. In contrast, shorter-tenured members have often learned to respond to individual needs and personal desires, and they value informal
worship that allows individual expression and different forms of participation from week to week, if not from moment to moment. The argument tends to be cast into which form of worship is "right" and which is
"wrong" or who will win and who will lose. The more subtle issue at the
heart of the difference, however, is that our parents have learned life
lessons about how to behave as a group (and therefore assume that what
is right for one person in worship is right for all), while our children
have learned life lessons about how to behave as individuals (and therefore assume that what is right is "what's right for me"). These cultural
and generational life teachings also shape what we expect from our banks,
our schools, our families, and our marketplace. Yet, when brought into
our congregations, they rest hidden under the surface, and we most often
have no language for the discomfort that separates us at a time when we
wish to be together in community.

Let us not paint too bleak a picture. There are, of course, healthy congregations, but many of them are anxious to stay healthy and realize that they will have to work to do so. It is not uncommon for leaders of healthy congregations to have their time and energy diverted by the necessity of "putting out fires" and "mending fences" as small controversies and seemingly inconsequential differences or preferences quickly bloom into disruptive problems. Often members are surprised that uncivil and sometimes damaging behavior gets lived out in their congregation, and often leaders are disappointed that they are not equipped to handle these situations better.

In her spiritual memoir entitled *Dakota*, Kathleen Norris reflects on the difference that she found between a Benedictine monastic community and a Protestant congregation in a small Dakota town. In both cases the people of these two religious communities were confronted with deep disagreements which severely divided them. In her example from the Benedictine community, she told of a group meeting that began and ended with prayer. As the participants talked about the positions that divided them, everyone spoke; everyone heard and gave counsel. The result was an agreement that allowed all of the participants to remain in the community without feeling compromised or defeated.

The example from the small Protestant congregation was quite different. A woman who was a member of that congregation was stunned to learn several days following a difficult woman's group meeting that a former teacher of hers, and a sister member of the congregation, had actively been criticizing her behind her back. Norris noted again, referring to the meeting at which the disagreement took place, that it also began and ended with prayer. This time, however, no one had a say, no one was heard, and community was diminished.

In reflecting on the differences Norris writes:

> One thing that distinguishes the monastery from the small town is that the Rule of St. Benedict, read aloud daily and constantly interpreted, provides definition of certain agreed-upon values that make for community. The small-town minister, expected to fill the role of such a rule by reminding people to love one another, is usually less effectual.[1]

Sadly, it does seem that despite the disciplines and resources which are available in each of our various faith traditions, many of our congregations are ill-equipped, poorly trained, or insufficiently motivated to translate the teachings of faith into daily practice. Occasional reminders in sermons or admonishments during committee meetings do not make a substantive difference. It is often the case that we lack the kind of community and dialogue which we hope would be found among people in congregations.

We are quite literally caught between the proverbial rock and the hard place. We wrestle uncomfortably with our differences and wish that they would disappear in consensus and congregational harmony. Yet, at the same time, we need our differences. In fact, the vitality and the life source of our faith depends upon our differences as we seek new ways to be authentic and faithful in a time of changing assumptions (so often talked about as "changing paradigms"). Ronald Heifetz, director of the Leadership Education Project at Harvard University, writes along with his colleague Donald Laurie, "Different people within the same organization bring different experiences, assumptions, values, beliefs, and habits to their work. This diversity is valuable *because innovation and learning are the products of differences* [emphasis added]."[2] We are in what has been widely recognized as a major turning point in our culture, a time that requires new learning for our congregations. In order to respond creatively and appropriately, we need disparate voices to sit around the decision-making tables in our congregations. Our response requires more than trying to tolerate or accommodate differences or trying to help people "fit" by conforming to the present norms. We actually need people to maintain their differences with integrity if we are to live into the future.

The importance of differences may be brought home a bit by a favorite example from outside the world of our congregations. While I can't recall where I heard or read this story, it has remained with me for a number of years because it includes all of the frustration and the ridicule that is too often heard in congregational conversations. Yet the insight that was so critical for this organization to move ahead came from a group of very different people who stayed in conversation when they didn't know what to do about their problem.

The problem was a recent mauling of an electric power line repair person by a bear. This apparently was not an infrequent hazard experienced by outdoor, line repair workers in a power utility company that

serviced this northern region where there was an abundance of snow. It
seemed that heavy snows would regularly knock down power lines, and
the repair workers sent out to correct the problem would be seen as a
potential food source by arctic bears needing food in the snowbound
conditions. A consultant was called to help find some remedy, and a
general meeting was called in which representatives from all quarters in
the organization were involved: upper management, office management,
line workers, technical workers, and office support personnel. After a
full morning's work no answer had been found and participants were a
bit terse with the consultant when told to go back into their small groups
in the afternoon with new instructions to "play" with ideas and seek new
insights. Obviously a number of people felt that the consultant was remiss in not producing an answer. (How often in our congregations are
leaders seen as remiss if they are not able to provide direct solutions to
baffling problems!)

Sometime in the midafternoon the critical insight hit. It came from
a playful and, for some, a ridiculous and time-wasting conversation in
which people used all of their differences. If I recall correctly, the conversation went something like this. One member began to talk face-
tiously about there being so many bears out in the areas where the power
company had to continually repair lines. Perhaps they ought to find a
way to get the bears to fix the lines so that the employees could stay
inside where it was warm and safe. One of the line workers, who had
seen a bear shaking the pole trying to get at a worker, laughed and suggested that the bear could solve the problem in another way. A bear is
so powerful that it could just shake the pole during a snowstorm and the
snow would fall from the overburdened lines. Others said that a bear
wouldn't shake the pole if there was no worker up on the pole to get it
interested. Another person chimed in to say that what was needed was
for the line workers to put a pot of honey on top of the pole instead of
workers. That would get the bear interested in shaking the pole. Yes,
countered another, but the workers would still have to be out there to
place the honey pots on the poles and they would still be attacked by the
bears. (Can't you just hear a conversation like this in which frustrated
members of your congregation are reduced to fancy, while others are
disgusted by the way time is being wasted?) One of the executives then
suggested that perhaps what they needed to do was to use the company
helicopters to distribute the honey. Yes, agreed one of the technical

workers. Instead of flying the big execs around for big bucks, they ought to use the helicopters after a storm to lower a honey pot to the top of every pole to attract the bears. And this is when the new learning occurred. One of the office managers said, "That's it! I used to be a nurse in an evacuation hospital in Vietnam and I'll never forget the noise and the commotion of the helicopters flying wounded soldiers in. The tents would flap and whole areas of the camp would jump with pounding air. We don't need honey and we don't need bears. We just need to fly helicopters close enough over the power lines to blow the snow off before the lines break, and then we won't have to send any repair workers into such dangerous situations." The creative next step had been found.

The point of the example above is that creative and innovative solutions are seldom discovered by people who are all alike and are all in agreement about the way things should be done. Creative and innovative solutions or steps are seldom discovered without some uncomfortable rambling about unusual or unorthodox ideas. Once we look at our situation through a well-established set of assumptions, it is difficult to see anything except what we have already seen, difficult to think anything that we have not already thought. The old saying that continues to keep coming back to me as I work with groups is "If all I have is a hammer, everything I see looks like a nail." In order to discover a creative response to a problem, we need people with all of their differences intact, who can collaboratively look at the life and ministry of our congregations in new ways. These people need to be mature and caring and be willing to listen to and honor others, thus reflecting the values and teachings of the faith that they share. We don't need competition or the search for winners and losers in the midst of our differences.

The context of our ministry is different than it was yesterday and requires new cultural languages and more culturally friendly practices if we want to invite others to share our faith with us. We are learning that we can't keep looking at our worship and at our congregations through the same lens of established assumptions and long-practiced traditions. So it is with us in faith communities just as it is with all other institutions and organizations in our changing culture.

I was intrigued by the words of a friend who has worked as a consultant to a marketing department of one of the major automobile companies and who was describing new learning about the difference between "push information" and "pull information." Push information is information that sales people or marketers push at the consumer in order to interest that person in the product. Marketers push information at us on TV and radio and more aggressively through unsolicited telemarketing during our evening meal. Not surprisingly, many consumers have become rather adept at fending off push information. Pull information, on the other hand, is information that people reach out and pull toward themselves because they are interested and because the information is timely for a decision or purchase they want to make. My consultant friend said that the automobile industry was trying to learn how to deal with this new context of defensive consumers who have well-established prejudices about aggressive sales people who push information at prospective consumers in order to get them to make decisions about a new car on the spot. In fact, he said, the automobile marketers were learning that one of the favorite times for many people to shop for a new car was when the dealership was closed. People could then walk around the cars on the lot and learn what they could about them without having sales people push information at them or push for a decision.

This insight about the new context of shoppers was leading automobile dealers to experiment with "pull information." Some dealers were experimenting with interactive information kiosks that would be placed outside on the lot and would be available 24 hours per day for off-hour browsers. Potential customers could visit the car lot at any hour and, using the kiosks, gather information on the cars they were interested in without having to deal with a salesperson. If the person was interested in a car, he or she could then return to talk with a salesperson and be better armed with information to make a decision.

If automobile dealers need to learn about the changing context of their market and the new behaviors of potential customers, it should be no surprise that leaders of congregations need to learn about present and future members of their congregations who have different needs regarding membership, worship, committee participation, and spiritual questions. We need people to come to worship, committee meetings, small groups, and governing boards with all of their differences intact. Attracting such people is not a question of marketing and getting enough new members to keep our congregations afloat (increasing market share); rather, it is about the living vibrancy of our faith that needs to continue to reshape itself if we are to be able to talk with new generations of people and be understood.

We need people who understand the historic roots of our worship practices and who can interpret those traditions, but we also need people who can explain why spontaneity and individual expression, which changes from week to week, is the way in which many people unfamiliar with traditional forms of worship will most easily engage God and the meaning of their faith. And we need all of these people in the same room at the same time, talking and listening to one another, in order for our faith traditions to live effectively in this changing context.

We need people who can explain why it is important for the pastor, priest, or rabbi to visit a member of the congregation who has been hospitalized; but we also need people who can explain why it is important and appropriate for that hospitalized person to be visited by another church member who has the gift of caring and nurture. And we need all of these people in the same room at the same time, talking and listening to one another, in order for our faith traditions to live effectively in this changing context.

We need people who can explain the importance for members of the congregation to serve on committees and to help organize and run the institution, but we also need people who can explain that committee work is not necessarily the same as faith work and that actions and activities on short-term task forces or activities outside of the congregation are equally important. And we need all of these people in the same room at the same time, talking and listening to one another, in order for our faith traditions to live effectively in this changing context.

Yes, such a mix of people with different understandings and expectations will engage our differences and it will, at times, be uncomfortable, but a vibrant and growing faith that speaks to the contemporary world is dependent upon it. "Part of the genius of congregations lies in their ability to express the particularity of a people," writes Dorothy Bass, Director of the Valparaiso Project on the Education and Formation of People in Faith, talking about the role of congregations as bearers of traditions that need to be shaped and formed in new ways to speak to the next generation in the specificity of their own unique context.[3] Quoting the work of philosopher Alasdair MacIntyre, Bass states that when a faith tradition is "'living'. . . its members are engaged in a vibrant, embodied 'argument,' stretching across time and space, about what the fullest participation in its particular goods would entail."[4]

Many of our congregations are not prepared to have that "vibrant, embodied argument" that will keep the faith alive and reshape it in order to pass it on to the next generation of seekers and practitioners. What Bass refers to as "arguments" are the skills of dialogue, of listening, and of learning. They mold our practices of the faith and keep them vital. Instead, too many of our congregations experience the form of argument that results in winners and losers. The conversations in our congregations too often seek to differentiate between those who see themselves as morally right and those who are seen to be morally bankrupt; between those who are wedded to traditionalism and those who don't even want to get "engaged" if it would mean submitting to any form of faith discipline; and between those who agree with the priest or rabbi and those who disagree with her or him. And all too often these win/lose arguments are accompanied by behaviors and attitudes that clearly do not reflect the values and practices of the faith. I will argue in this book that in many of our arguments in congregations we have defaulted to community tactics of trying to win instead of listening, and that it is all too difficult to distinguish between an argument in a congregation and an argument at a zoning board hearing or a public school board meeting where participants are interested in winning at any cost. This is a problem that we can understand if we look at the bigger picture of our culture. It is also a problem that we can, and should, do something about as communities that are meant to reflect our faith traditions and our relationship with God.

About This Book

This book is a continuation of the final chapter of my previous book *Leading Change in the Congregation: Spiritual and Organizational Tools for Leaders*. In that book I sought to introduce leaders to dynamics of congregational change and to help them diagnose what was happening in the congregation and what the appropriate leadership response or responses might be. It was based on the premise that congregations need to deal continuously with change, change both internal and external to the congregation, and it acknowledged that when congregations experience change, anxiety increases. I wrote:

> Change increases anxiety. People who feel pushed into change

respond with active resistance as they seek to restore an equilibrium that seems threatened. The give and take, the push and pull, is not always gracious. Surprised people tend to behave badly.[5]

In that final chapter I recognized the increased incivility that has infused not only our culture but our congregations as well. I called for a reclaiming and renewing of our sense that we live under covenants with others which allow and require us to share our faith by behaving in loving ways toward each other. Living in loving ways is not meant to be practiced only to the point at which we confront differences and disagreements. It is meant to be practiced through and beyond those disagreements, as we live together toward community.

It is significant to note that real community is created by working through disagreements, not by going around them and not by denying that they are real. Scott Peck, who is a psychiatrist, author, and lecturer, names four stages in order: pseudocommunity, chaos, emptiness, and community.[6] Groups begin in a pseudocommunity, an easy togetherness in which they try to be pleasant with one another and avoid all disagreements. In describing this as pseudocommunity, Peck notes quite frankly, "It never works." In order to move toward genuine community in which there is both peace and connection with others, the members need to move through chaos and emptiness. Yet the chaos and the emptiness can be frightening and disorienting. The chaos and emptiness often surprise people who assume congregations are fully harmonious places where everyone is, or is supposed to be, happy. And, as I said, surprised people tend to behave badly.

In a culture that is increasingly becoming known for its incivility, we in religious faith communities are exceptionally well-grounded in disciplines and traditions that will enable us to move through chaos and emptiness together if we practice what we have inherited. We need to rediscover and begin to learn and follow disciplines of covenantal behaviors that are consistent with other practices of our faith. As Kathleen Norris points out, we need to do more than have our clergy offer ineffectual general reminders for people to love one another. Community in the practice of faith is more demanding than that. It is more disciplined than that.

This book is an attempt to take several steps toward honoring and living with the differences that are ours and which we need for our future. It is an attempt to help congregations reclaim some of the disciplines and traditions that will help in a time of change. Although I offer some theoretical explanation about the current situation in North American congregations, the real concern of this book is to help move our congregations from understanding to action. More than a description of why agreement and community are difficult in our congregations in the present moment, this book is intended to provide a resource for congregations that seek to remain as communities despite, and because of, their differences. This book attempts to address the question, "How will we live together in our differences?"

How To Use This Book

As the title suggests, this book is meant to be a handbook for action. It offers understanding, resources, and a basic strategy to move from ideas to action. Attention will not be given to trying to find the "right" answer to any issue or situation that a congregation is facing. Instead, this book will give attention to why and how we can agree to live and act together as we search for the right answers or for the next steps to present themselves to our congregations.

The Background Theory (Chapters 1 and 2)

This theory looks at the bigger picture of our situation. The clergy and the key leaders of congregations need to have this kind of background. It is interpretive information, and the key leaders of congregations are interpreters. One of the primary functions of leaders is to be able to tell stories and to interpret situations in a way that helps people see themselves and sense what is an appropriate next step. Leaders need to be able to stand in the midst of a situation and bring meaning to people's experience. They need to provide the background to help others move beyond finger pointing and blame.

Key leaders also need to be able to depersonalize their own experiences when appropriate. Being in the path of someone's displeasure, or trying to lead in the midst of competing differences, is always uncomfortable. Not being able to satisfy the wishes of others and not being able to provide clear and simple solutions are difficult for leaders. When caught in that spot, which is common for leaders today, they need to understand that some of the critique, blame, and uncivil treatment that they receive and witness is as much a cultural expression as it is a direct result of their action.

Key leaders also need to understand the opportunity and responsibility they have to change and constrain their own behavior and to guide their congregations *before* everyone is mired in the push and pull of preferences and disagreements. A leader's task is, in part, a matter of learning conflict techniques; but it is also a matter of addressing the spiritual maturity of the congregation and inviting individuals and the congregation as a whole to take a step forward, to move beyond cultural practices, and to do so because of the shared faith that brings them together.

While everyone in the congregation may not need, or be interested in, the theory behind uncivil congregational behavior, leaders need to be able to understand the natural and expected sources of blaming and win/lose behaviors that they will encounter. It is highly recommended that the key leaders of a congregation read chapters 1 and 2.

The Basic Strategy: Behavioral Covenants (Chapter 3)

The purpose of this handbook is to lead congregations toward healthy behavior. The basic strategy of establishing behavioral covenants in congregations will be described in the third chapter. A behavioral covenant is a written document developed by leaders, agreed to and owned by its creators, and practiced on a daily basis as a spiritual discipline. It is a way of developing common language, common commitments, and an awareness of healthy behaviors. Each of our denominations, associations, or movements has documents to describe what precepts of faith are to be held central and what behaviors are to be practiced (or not practiced). Many of our congregations have behavioral covenants tucked away in their books of polity or denominational journals. These documents, however, have been written by other people in another time. While they are key documents for understanding ourselves and for forming commitments to our beliefs and behaviors, the individual congregation needs to shape the covenants in ways that can be owned and applied in the immediate setting. Chapter 3 will introduce behavioral covenants as a functional tool for guiding healthy and faithful behavior.

Where "The Rubber Meets the Road": Ideas and Resources for Working with Your Congregation (Chapter 4 and Resource Section)

The final two sections of this book will offer meeting designs and resources for working with your congregation to understand cultural incivility and ways to choose to behave differently from the cultural default. They will offer strategies for developing behavioral covenants to guide people in the congregation. Chapter 4 offers four modules for working with congregational leaders in different settings:

- A one-and-a-half-day leadership retreat
- A one-day leadership retreat
- A series of five 20-minute components for regular board or committee meetings
- Four meetings with a leadership team with the specific ad hoc responsibility of working with congregational behavior

The resource section has a series of resources to be used along with the modules designed in chapter 4. The first resource in that section, "Holy Manners: The Spiritual Politeness of Healthy Congregations," is an abbreviated statement or an "executive summary" of the initial chapters of this book. It is designed to be photocopied and distributed to the leaders of your congregation in order to provide an overview for the work of developing behavioral covenants. Encouraging your leaders to read this resource in advance of conversations about your own congregation will offer a bigger picture and more balanced context for understanding and leading your congregation.

When the "rubber hits the road," it is important to work with the specific needs, preferences, and behaviors of your own congregation. The modules and the resources offered can be used as presented, but they can, and perhaps should, be modified and adapted to fit your own congregation. Permission is freely given for you to change and adapt the ideas and resources found in these sections. All the resources in this final section of the book are reproducible and can be photocopied for your use with your congregation.

Notes

1. Kathleen Norris, *Dakota: A Spiritual Geography* (New York: Houghton Mifflin Co., 1993), 115-116.

2. Ronald A. Heifetz and Donald L. Laurie, "The Work of Leadership" *Harvard Business Review* (January-February 1997): 128.

3. Dorothy C. Bass, "Congregations and the Bearing of Traditions" in *American Congregations* by James Wind and James W. Lewis (eds.), vol. 2 (Chicago: The University of Chicago Press, 1994): 170.

4. Ibid., 172.

5. Gil Rendle, *Leading Change in the Congregation: Spiritual and Organizational Tools for Leaders* (Bethesda, Md.: The Alban Institute), 160.

6. M. Scott Peck, *The Different Drum: Community Making and Peace* (New York: Simon and Schuster, 1987), 86.

CHAPTER 1

Understanding Uncivil Behavior— The Bigger Picture

"Wait! Stop the meeting!" We were about 30 minutes into a meeting of key congregational leaders that had begun without the minister, who was unexplainably absent. But here he was, storming in the door and waving a piece of paper over his head. "Wait! Stop the meeting," he said, "and read this!" He handed me a letter from his lawyer which named one of the trustees who was present at the meeting and instructed that he was no longer to set foot on the minister's parsonage property (owned by the church) and was no longer to make any unsolicited phone calls to the parsonage at any time of the day. The letter identified the next legal steps that would be taken if the named trustee did not comply with the letter.

How is it that a minister turned to the strategy of talking with a problematic parishioner through a lawyer's letter rather than face to face? Yet, this is not an isolated instance of difficult behavior in a congregation. For example, in another congregation the pastor made repeated attempts to deal with an aggrieved member who was working actively to have the pastor removed from leadership. Each time the pastor met that member face to face, however, he was greeted by a smile, pleasantries, and little or no hint of a problem. In another congregation, a governing board asked their consultant to present its report to a full meeting of the congregation. This was done to prevent the personal accusations and name-calling that board members had experienced in the last several congregational meetings. And in yet another, four members of a 14-member governing board held clandestine meetings to which they did not invite the other board members and during which they planned a strategy for ridding themselves of their clergy leader. Somehow they managed not to feel disloyal to the rest of the board members or to the congregation, which they represented. What sense can one make of a congregational member who sends in hundreds of dollars worth of unwanted magazine subscriptions filled out with the name and address of his or her clergy, as an expression of anger with that leader? Beside being illegal, how is this different from the congregational member who won't talk to another member because she's "on the wrong side" of an issue, or the rabbi who won't fulfill a public commitment he made to a capital fund campaign because he didn't receive the salary increment that he felt was his due?

Perhaps most disconcerting is the fact that most readers will not be surprised to know that all of these are real examples from real congregations. Examples of uncivil behavior that falls outside the teachings of the faith are fairly common in the experience of too many congregational leaders–clergy and laity alike. These stories are disconcerting, to be sure, and ill behavior such as this, when encountered in the congregation, often makes members or leaders wonder why they have committed themselves to this faith community and if they should continue that commitment. Frequently, the experiences of uncivil behavior are more subtle or common than the examples above. It is more likely that members will be disturbed by unkind public comments overheard in the congregation; by the spreading of rumors and gossip; by the use of anonymous information to question the decisions or actions of leaders; by the public finger-pointing when something goes wrong; or by the attribution of negative, rather than positive, motives to somebody's actions.

Should our congregations be different from these startling or common examples of uncivil behavior? Should we expect the behavior of members of faith communities to be more responsible, more caring, and more faithful? The answer is definitely yes! In fact, helping our congregations to move toward more responsible and faithful behavior is the very focus and purpose of this book. I will argue, as I mentioned, that many of the people in our congregations, indeed, in many congregations, have "defaulted" to the behaviors of our culture and need to be called back to behaviors that belong to faith communities. Before we get to that point, however, it is important to understand the larger context in which this less-than-faithful behavior is happening in our congregations. What we experience as uncivil or irresponsible behavior in our congregations often has a history and an origin outside of the congregation. The examples shared at the beginning of the chapter don't belong just to congregations. Similar things happen in neighborhoods, community meetings, businesses, banks, hospitals, and friendships as well. Incivility is part of a bigger picture that can be seen from a number of very interesting perspectives. Telling the story of the bigger picture, however, does not excuse, condone, minimize, or dismiss the uncivil and uncaring behavior that occurs in many of our congregations. But knowing something about the context of our congregational stories is necessary in order for congregational leaders to respond appropriately when less than civil behavior is experienced in their own congregations.

Depersonalizing the Bumps and Bruises

Much of what happens to leaders in congregations is a product of, and belongs to, the larger system of persons, norms, and practices of the congregation as a whole, or of the community or cultural context that surrounds the congregation. These contextual variables would be present no matter who the leader is or what the leader does. Indeed, one of the tasks of congregational leadership is to try to distinguish which actions, responses, or consequences "belong to" the person of the leader and which belong to the whole system of the congregation. In other words, it is important for leaders to know and to understand, to whatever degree possible, what part of that which they experience or observe is a consequence of the leader's own behavior (or misbehavior) and what part is a consequence of the context in which the congregational system already exists.

Not to try to distinguish between the consequences of our own behavior and the natural consequences of the congregational system or the context in which the congregation does ministry means that the leader(s) will always feel responsible, and be held responsible, for everything that happens. In good times, when things go well, this misplaced responsibility is not usually perceived to be a problem. Leaders are happy to claim the good results as a product of their actions. For example, I recently worked with a congregation that had doubled its worship attendance. The congregation was located in one of the fastest growing counties in the United States, and the population around this congregation was both growing and "turning over" as a large number of mobile families came and went quickly in the growing community. The fact was that the leaders of this congregation would have had to work hard *not* to grow, given the circumstances surrounding them. However, the reality of the situation was that the leaders–clergy and laity alike– did their home-work and worked hard at invitation and inclusion. The congregation grew, and no one distinguished between whether the results were due to the good work and faithful leadership of the clergy and their board or to the community context, which was forever feeding new people into their worship services.

In less than good times, however, to fail to distinguish between the product of our own behavior and the product of the congregational sys-tem, or the context in which the congregation does ministry, means that leaders will always be blamed, or will blame themselves, for unwanted outcomes. It is common practice in organizations for people to want to know what went wrong when desired outcomes are not achieved. When it is not possible to identify what went wrong, people quickly shift to asking who was wrong. Since ours is a complex world and it is difficult to find clear explanations for the one or two "whats" that go wrong, it does not take long for the question to shift from "what?" to "who?" In a setting in which people are disappointed that their idealized outcome was not achieved, the leader needs to be clear about which results, or lack of results, rest on his or her own choices or behaviors, and which rest on the larger congregational system or on the context in which the congregation exists.

For example, in another consultation with a congregation I discov-ered a very gifted and perceptive clergy leader and a good number of thoughtful lay leaders who were already asking the right questions and taking rather creative and risky steps. But their location, the size and condition of their facilities, the median age of the membership, and the changing neighborhood in which fewer and fewer of their neighbors spoke the same language and shared the congregation's traditions sug-gested that, despite their creative and thoughtful leadership, their con-gregation may have a very short future. The situation was already critical. The internal situation of the congregation was also ripe for members to turn to their clergy leader and blame her for not having the answers to their problems, for not being a charismatic enough preacher to attract people to the congregation, or for not working long enough, or hard enough, to make the critical difference. The situation was also ripe for members to turn to some of their long-term leaders and blame them for holding on to old patterns and traditions for too long and not allowing new leaders and new ideas to take hold. This was a congregation that had already demonstrated its interest in pointing out what was wrong with its leaders. In fact, they describe their present difficult situation in terms of what the last two clergy leaders did *not* do to make it different. If their present attempts and strategic choices do not produce the people and the dollars needed to sustain the life of their congregation, they are already poised to blame their current leaders. This is a case in which leaders and members alike need to differentiate between the results produced by their leaders and the results produced by their context. In a time when we allow widespread blame and less than civil confrontation, not to distinguish between these personal and contextual differences means that the leader will unrealistically assume all blame.

Even when we try to distinguish between personal and contextual differences, people tend to personalize. We take things personally, and we accuse personally. We easily assign blame to people rather than seek multiple causes or try to understand complex interrelationships that influence the situation we are facing. We move quickly to conclusions such as "I must have done something wrong" or "He is wrong in what he did." Whenever we run into behaviors such as blaming, the passing of rumors and innuendo, or conversations behind people's backs, it seems that there is a natural invitation to personalize the experience. Leaders forever ask, "Why would someone do that to me?" or "What have I done to deserve such treatment?" But the fact is that there is a much larger cultural context for the difficult behavior that is found in many of our congregations. It goes well beyond the personal.

In all such situations leaders need to learn to differentiate between themselves and the congregations in which they provide leadership. In his classic work *Generation to Generation,* Edwin Friedman, noted rabbi and teacher of family systems theory as applied to congregations, writes of differentiation as the capacity to define one's life's goals and values apart from surrounding pressures toward "togetherness."[1] One needs to be able to see and understand himself or herself apart from the whole congregation, even while being a part of the congregation, and especially when taking on the critical role of leader in the congregation. Friedman talks about leaders developing the capacity to maintain a "nonanxious presence" in anxious systems such as many of our congregations have become. In order to be nonanxious, leaders have to learn to

take responsibility for what belongs to them, and to not take responsibility for actions or results that do not belong to them or for which they are
not responsible, even when the congregation wants to point the finger of
blame and insist that they take responsibility. Being able to maintain the
position of a nonanxious leader is critical. As Friedman wrote, "The
capacity of [leaders] to contain their own anxiety regarding congregational matters, both those not related to them, as well as those where
they become the identified focus, may be the most significant capability
in their arsenal."[2] Leaders need to know when they are receiving or level-
ing complaints and expressing concerns that are justified and appropriate, and when they are receiving or practicing uncivil or inappropriate
behavior that is presently supported by the cultural landscape. In addition, leaders need to know that when they practice or receive less than
caring criticism, it may be more about the current cultural practice of
individuals who are pushing their own preferences in a battle assumed to
have winners and losers than it is about the leaders' own ineffectiveness.

Not to know how to differentiate between oneself and the larger
picture in which one is living can be exceedingly painful. For example,
I think in particular about one young man who graduated from seminary
and began work as the pastor of a small, urban congregation in which
most of the members were blue-collar workers. The members were deeply
committed to their congregation and deeply concerned about its future,
which was at some risk. As in many blue-collar congregations, when
people talked, they did not mince words, but spoke very directly and
pointedly to one another and to their new pastor. When they were in
board meetings, it was common for more than one person to speak at a
time, and decisions were often made by several people talking simulta-
neously. When people made a point, they often literally pointed with
their fingers for emphasis. Their new young pastor—a person who had
grown up in a quiet professional family, had gone from college straight
to seminary, had never held a job outside of the church, and was a very
quiet spirit—could not differentiate between when his congregational
leaders were yelling (speaking with energy) and when they were yelling
at him. He personalized every encounter and was never able to differentiate himself and his performance as minister from what he perceived as
criticism directed at him from the congregation. Before the second year
of his tenure, the young minister left not only his leadership role with
that congregation but his role as a clergy person as well. As my good

friend and pastoral counselor Jerry Rardin often notes, quoting his therapeutic trainer Yvonne Agazarian, "If you take it personally, you will suffer more."

Being self-differentiated–being able to distinguish between one's own self and what is going on in the congregation or the culture–is not an easy task. It is very difficult in highly complex settings to know and to be clear about what is due to one's own efforts and what is part and product of the whole congregation or its setting. Compounding the reality of the complexity of most of our situations is the propensity for many leaders in churches and synagogues to be people-oriented and, as "people people," naturally to take things personally. Relationships are the currency of work in congregations, and people in congregations are hypersensitive to relationships and to both accusations and innuendos of blame.

How then do leaders understand and depersonalize some of the uncaring and uncivil behavior that can be found in so many congregations, as the examples at the beginning of this chapter attest? One helpful way to depersonalize and to differentiate is to understand the big picture–the cultural context in which it becomes evident that the disturbing behavior that we find in our congregations is to some degree prevalent in and a product of our current culture. Without excusing uncivil behavior and without minimizing its destructiveness, leaders need to have some sense of the roots and the pervasiveness of the confrontational and competitive behavior that is being practiced in our culture. Mature and responsible leaders need to know when and how to make the significant shift from asking "Why is this happening to me?" to asking "Why is this such common behavior for all of us?" Leaders in faith communities need a big enough picture to have some understanding of the prevalence and the causes of uncivil behavior and behavior inappropriate to healthy community so that they can stop asking the personal question of "Why are these people doing this to me?" and help the whole congregation to ask, "Is this the way we would want our faith community to behave?"

The Big Picture

Individual and daily behavior in our homes, our workplaces, our neighborhoods, and our congregations takes its shape and follows patterns set by larger social movements. Ours is not the first time in which people decry the lack of civility and the loss of respectful behavior. For example, in the late 1800s Americans were noted for their bad manners and uncivil behavior, including behavior by theater audiences who regularly hissed at bad performers and tossed fruit and eggs to chase them from the stage. During that period in our national life, disagreements often exploded into violence, even to the point of a member of the United States House of Representatives using a cane to beat Senator Charles Sumner senseless.[3] Ours is not the first time in which the antihero is celebrated in the arts and in which asserting individual rights and wants is sanctioned above the needs of others. Given these earlier social periods of uncivil behavior, it is not surprising to note that the kind of individual confrontation and blaming that occurs so easily in many of our congregations has been prevalent at other times, even though it was unheard of 40 years ago and would have been less prevalent 20 years ago than it is today.

One of the ways to describe the larger picture of our current cultural and congregational experience is in a cyclical telling of history. Historians William Strauss and Neil Howe tell our national story in terms of the cycle of generations. They describe cycles that shift and repeat certain driving values and behaviors beginning in European history and extending throughout American history as dominant forces that shape both people and events. It is provocative that the subtitle of one of their books is *The History of America's Future, 1584 to 2069*, indicating that cycles that began hundreds of years ago will continue to direct our story in the future.[4] Looking at generational periods of approximately 22 years, Strauss and Howe describe generational "constellations" that each carry their own character and influence. As they state, "Whenever the constellation shifts up by one notch, the behavior and attitudes of each phase of life change character entirely."[5]

According to their description, we are now in the third phase of the current repetition of a recurring pattern of four cycles.[6] The four cycles include a "high," an "awakening," an "unraveling," and a "crisis." The three particular cycles that we need to focus on for our discussion include:

- HIGH

A high begins when society perceives that the basic issues of a prior crisis have been resolved. The prior crisis whose resolution began the most immediate high that we need to explore was World War II. The "American High" was the consolidation of our nation following the war and, as identified by Strauss and Howe, lasted from 1946 to 1964.

- AWAKENING

An awakening begins when events trigger a revolution in the culture and the awakening is designed to compensate or correct what is felt to be missing in the high. Strauss and Howe identify our most recent awakening as the "Consciousness Revolution" of 1964 to 1984.

- UNRAVELING

An unraveling is the phase that consolidates and formalizes the new direction uncovered by the awakening, and it stands in contrast, or as a polar opposite, to the high. According to Strauss and Howe, the current unraveling that we are experiencing began in 1984 and they have given it the name "Culture Wars."

While these repeating cycles of crisis–high, awakening, unraveling–are traced by Strauss and Howe with almost uninterrupted repetition from the Western European Renaissance in the last quarter of the fifteenth century to the current day, glimpses of the recurring cycles can be seen well before that in biblical literature and in early Greek mythology. Each of these generational periods carries its own markers and values. Some of these generational turnings help to describe why our congregations, our families, and our public lives are as filled with as much uncivil behavior as they seem to be.

As one would imagine, the high of the post World War II years brought with it a recommitment to the life of the community. People put the crisis of war behind them and worked together as a group to build a neighborhood and a society that was purposeful and secure. Following the experience of war there was a high demand for order and consensus. Security and predictability were valued, and any public argument (in the marketplace as well as in the congregation) was over means, not over ends. While people might quibble over how to do things, it was assumed that everyone understood and worked for common ends and shared goals. Conformity was at its height in the home, in the workplace, and in the congregation. It was less likely that confrontation would break out in congregational meetings or that subgroups of members would strategize against other subgroups in order to get their way. The supported assumption was that the congregation had one, often unstated, purpose or goal. And while there might be debate about the best means of getting to the goal, once the goal was agreed on, it was expected that each person would pull his or her weight in common endeavor. For example, there might have been debate about how the annual financial campaign was to be conducted or who would lead it, but there was no question about whether members would support it.

A common current distinction that is often made to differentiate between *leadership* and *management* states that "managers do things right, leaders do the right things."[7] In other words, the function of management is to make sure things are done correctly, because the end or the goal is assumed to be correct. The role of management is to make things go smoothly and to pay attention to *how* things are done, not *why* they are done. In contrast, leaders need to ask questions about purpose and about whether or not what is being done is right and is being done for the right reasons. Leaders unsettle people when they ask foundational questions of purpose and goal. Managers tend to stabilize people and organizations by directing people to do things right, that is, in harmony and with conformity. During the post World War II high that Strauss and Howe describe, in which conformity and goals of progress were widely shared, the predominant work of the governing boards of churches and synagogues was management more than leadership. In a cultural time of building and expanding all institutions, leaders in our congregations depended upon the harmony of groups which shared a common cause and in which disagreement and dissent were not encouraged. Many of the congregational battles and much of the divisive behavior that is experienced in our congregations today would have been highly out of place in churches and synagogues just a few decades ago. It is no surprise that the post World War II years into the 1960s were remembered as a time of growth, energy, and harmony, because they were. Describing this most recent national high, Strauss and Howe write:

We brimmed over with optimism about Camelot, a bustling future with smart people in which big projects and "impossible dreams" were freshly achievable. The moon could be reached and poverty eradicated, both within a decade. Tomorrowland was a friendly future with moving sidewalks, pastel geometric shapes, soothing Muzak, and well-tended families.[8]

But even as civilized, conforming behaviors were strengthened during the high, and as security and progress were increasingly achieved, generations naturally began to shift. An emerging generation began to question the lack of spirit and energy in a highly conformist society, spirit and energy that had been exhibited during the preceding crisis. While the post World War II high benefited from the stability and conformity of a culture that encouraged people to see themselves as part of the *group,* it also experienced a certain staleness of spirit and energy for *individuals.* Although many demographers and historians have looked at the baby-boom phenomenon as a function of the size of that new generation, Strauss and Howe see the shifting values which came with baby boomers who were more interested in a cultural awakening that challenged the order, purposefulness, and conformity of their predecessor generation. Their spiritual expressions and social ideals challenged and competed with the previous generation's assumption that progress requires individuals to defer to the group. The American experience was leaving the high behind and moving ahead to a cycle of exploration, the new awakening. As Strauss and Howe describe this movement, "Society searches for soul over science, meanings over things. Youth-fired attacks break out against the established institutional order. As these attacks take their toll, society has difficulty coalescing around common goals. People stop believing that social progress requires social discipline. Any public effort that requires collective discipline encounters withering controversy."[9] When once people might have debated over means, they now argued publicly and proficiently over ends. Liberating cultural forces kicked in, and individuals began to see themselves as distinct from the group. No longer was the argument over the appropriate way to run a stewardship campaign in the congregation. Now the argument was over why a person should be a member of a congregation at all. Conformity gave way to individual expression and exploration. The stability and conformity of the group naturally gave way to the competition and confrontation among individuals who now sought personal expression with complete freedom.

As I mentioned, this bigger picture can be drawn in several different ways, each of which helps us to understand the movement in our larger cultural context that currently both permits and practices less-than-civil, and often less-than-healthy, behavior. The big picture, as we are drawing it here, is enriched by the seminal work of Daniel Yankelovich, founder and president of Yankelovich, Skelly & White, Inc. and one of America's most respected analysts of social trends and public attitudes. Yankelovich points to the "cultural values" which rest at the very foundation of our daily behaviors as a people, and his work suggests that our cultural values have indeed shifted in this progression of generations that Strauss and Howe write about. We began in the World War II period (and well before) with an experience of shared, cultural values which Yankelovich referred to as a "giving/getting compact" based on the principle of deferred pleasure. Yankelovich describes the giving/getting compact as follows:

> I give hard work, loyalty, and steadfastness. I swallow my frustrations and suppress my impulses to do what I would enjoy, and do what is expected instead. I do not put myself first; I put the needs of others ahead of my own. I give a lot, but what I get in return is worth it. I receive an ever growing standard of living and a family life with a devoted spouse and decent kids. Our children will take care of us in our old age if we really need it, which thank goodness we will not. I have a nice home, a good job, the respect of my friends and neighbors; a sense of accomplishment at having made something of my life. Last, but not least, as an American I am proud to be a citizen of the finest country in the world.[10]

The principles of deferred pleasure, often referred to as the Protestant work ethic or the American dream because of the way in which the western European and early American Protestant experience so dominated the early history and development of the United States, reached their fullest strength in the World War II crisis. Americans came home from battlefields, where deferring pleasure and sacrificing individual preferences and desires to the will and need of the group/team/troop/nation had been practiced dramatically, successfully, and winningly. Because these experiences of deferred pleasure sounded so much like faith principles and could be so easily translated into and found within faith practices, the principles of deferred pleasure were often seen as synonymous with sharing a faith with others, as well as sharing a national identity. For example, the practice of an individual sacrificing personal satisfaction for the needs and benefits of others sounded consistent with the New Testament teachings about the "first being last." Self-sacrifice made perfect sense to people familiar with the conversation between Jesus and the disciples who were told to drop the familiarity of their fishing nets to "come follow" in order to serve the greater purpose of becoming fishers of men. Self-sacrifice made perfect sense to people familiar with the conversation between Jesus and the rich young ruler who was told that, in order to follow Jesus, perfection meant selling all that he had and giving it to the poor.

Undergirded by the cultural values of deferred pleasure and the sense of the importance of the group, and undergirded by the sense of conformity and purposefulness of working together for progress that was driven by the post World War II high, values of harmony and cohesiveness rested deep within our congregations. Individuals were expected to conform to the needs and practices of the congregation, not the other way around. It was a time of sameness in which congregations and synagogues of the same denomination or movement all worshiped, structured, and programmed themselves like all of the other congregations and synagogues in their denomination. As noted above, the driving management question for most congregational leaders was not "Are we doing what we believe God calls us to do?" but rather, "Are we doing right (to the best of our ability) what we believe God expects all congregations like ours to do?" In that environment it was expected that individuals would cooperate, not compete. Accepted norms of behavior involved collaboration, not confrontation. The expectations of leaders, and the behaviors of leaders and members alike, stressed cohesion and fair play.

Yankelovich puts a descriptive finger on a fundamental cultural value shift that we experienced in our national life and in our congregational lives. This shift changed many of the post World War II expectations of people, as well as our behavior. Pointing to the post-war economic shift in which individuals, communities, and the whole nation moved into a high level of production and development to catch up from the deferments imposed by a world war, Yankelovich states that the Protestant work ethic was undermined by capitalism itself:

The single greatest engine in the destruction of the Protestant work ethic was the invention of the installment plan, or instant credit. Previously one had to save in order to buy. But with credit cards one could indulge in instant gratification.[11]

Returning soldiers were anxious to defer no longer, but to catch up on life. The economic need to generate goods and to develop a means for instant ownership of those goods in order to supply these soldiers led to a shift in cultural values *from deferred pleasure to instant gratification*. Where once communities had "relational credit" in which a person could have a pound of hamburger today for which he or she would gladly repay on Tuesday because he or she knew the butcher, now a whole generation of people had instant credit to supply their needs and wishes, credit that was simply based on assumptions of future ability to pay. Of great significance was the shift not just of satisfaction and reward from the future to the present, but equally of group identity to individual identity. No longer did one defer individual desires for the sake of the larger group. Now the individual was the central entity to which the group would have to defer.

In the shift away from the central principle of deferred pleasure, we have traveled first through the Now Generation of the 1960s, through the Me Generation of the 1970s, and through the Generation of Greed of the 1980s, so named by the popular press. In a very brief period of time, which has been accompanied by the greatest increase of information ever known to humanity, we have gone through a kaleidoscopic change that has moved us further away from a group identity focused on conformity and sameness to a time highly sensitive to the individual. Our sociological analyses of America continue to describe us as a people who have become *consumers*, not deferrers. We ought not be surprised by, nor underestimate the importance of, cultural slogans such as, "If it feels good, do it," which point to the individual as the final arbiter of what is right and what is good for the individual. It is a mark of how far we have come from the assumption that "the good" is found in group identity, deferred pleasure, and the Protestant work ethic, an assumption with which so many of our congregational leaders comfortably began their lives in congregations.

Loren Mead offers another framework for the big picture in his popular description of the paradigm shift from the "Christendom paradigm" to a new, emerging, and yet not fully defined paradigm in which our congregations are living at the moment.[12] The sameness that was being described by the conformity of the high (Strauss and Howe) and the cohesion of deferred pleasure (Yankelovich) was also supported by the dominant cultural assumptions about the purpose of churches, synagogues, and congregational life.

What Loren Mead calls the Christendom paradigm began in A.D. 313 with the conversion of the Emperor Constantine to Christianity.[13] When he converted, everyone in the empire converted, and there was an assumed and enforced sameness among all people that made being a Christian and being a citizen one. As Mead states:

> The critical difference, once this paradigm settled in, was that by law the church was identified with the Empire. The world–the world that immediately surrounded the church–was legally identified with the church. There was no separation between world and church within the Empire. The law removed the hostility from the environment but also made the environment and the church identical.[14]

If anything, this period of Christendom, which has continued now for almost 1700 years, has been a time of sameness within the community and the congregation. To be a good member of a congregation and to be a good citizen have often been considered to be one and the same.

> Within the Empire there could be no distinction between sacred and secular. Bishops were leaders in things we might call secular (raising and deploying armies and playing major political roles, largely as stabilizing forces); kings and princes were leaders in things we might call religious (calling religious convocations and influencing their theological outcomes, just as the Emperor Constantine did at the Council of Nicea in 325).[15]

While this description of the bigger picture has largely been in the language of the Protestant church, its effect has been fully felt within Catholic and Jewish congregations as well. It has commonly been acknowledged in our own American history that, while our civic understanding has never allowed for an established religion, the mainline Protestant denominations established themselves early on as the dominant voice in North American public discourse. As writer James Davison Hunter states, "Cultural conflict is ultimately about the struggle for domination."[16] For the better part of our American history and for the earlier stages of many of our own personal histories, the mainline Protestant voice was the winner of cultural conflict and the dominant voice in the interpretation of our cultural standards and practices. While that has largely begun to change in more recent decades, mainline Protestant behavior and American civic behavior were understood to be similar, if not the same.

The bigger picture, described from any number of perspectives, is the story of one generation over and against the other. It is the story of one set of values, practices, and behaviors supplanting another set that served an earlier time well, but is now felt to be inadequate to today's task. While at the heart of the shift were changing assumptions about whether the group or the individual is more important—whether conformity or diversity, or stability or change, is to be embraced—the story is most often told and experienced as one generation of people against another. Classically, in our own time, the shift has been felt as a generation gap that separated GI parents from their baby-boom children. As Strauss and Howe describe it, "The emerging Boomer agenda was a deliberate antithesis to everything the prototypical G.I. male has stressed during the high: spiritualism over science, gratification over patience, fractiousness over conformity, rage over friendliness, negativism over positivism—and especially self over community."[17]

The generation gap and rivaling cultural values combined to create cultural forces that were liberating for the individual. These forces were embraced as society moved toward an unraveling, the third of the most recent turnings of the historical cycles, which Strauss and Howe identify as Culture Wars (1984-2005?).[18] Ours is a time marked by the celebration of individualism and the ebbing of public trust in a fragmented culture. It is a time of harsh debates over public values and practices. We should not be surprised that so many of our denominations and movements are engaged in highly conflicted and confrontational division over value-laden and scriptural issues such as abortion and homosexuality. *Culture Wars: The Struggle to Define America*[19] by Professor of Sociology and Religious Studies at the University of Virginia, James Davison Hunter, is an excellent resource for understanding not just the surface issues such as the family, education, media and the arts, law, electoral politics, and sexuality, but also the underlying value conflicts that support ongoing and seemingly irresolvable debates about these issues. At the heart of our arguments over prayer in public schools, over abortion and the right to life, and over homosexuality are contested values and assumptions of both spiritual and public nature. We no longer seek consensus as a guiding marker, as might have been done during a period of a high. Instead, the current cycle is marked by an individualism that seeks to win a debate, often without concern for civility and manners.

This period of unraveling following the awakening of the Consciousness Revolution is a time of weakened civic habits in which the individual no longer serves the needs of society; rather, an obliging society is seen as serving purposeful individuals. Our consumer-oriented society has trained individuals to be both aware of and responsive to their own needs, wants, and preferences, and people find it difficult to develop a sense of community. In a definitive article that has helped to shape much of the dialogue about the current state of public life, Robert Putnam, Dillon Professor of International Affairs at Harvard University, notes "striking evidence . . . that the vibrancy of American civil society has notably declined over the past several decades."[20] Reflecting on hundreds of studies in a dozen disparate disciplines, Putnam identifies a decline in "social capital," by which he means "features of social organization such as networks, norms, and social trust that facilitate coordination and cooperation for mutual benefit."[21] Whimsically, Putnam titles his article "Bowling Alone" to reflect the fact that more Americans are bowling today than ever before, but they are bowling alone rather than joining organized bowling leagues. The number of leagues has plummeted in the last decade, just as has the number of people who participate in religious congregations, civic organizations such as the Boy Scouts and Red Cross, and fraternal organizations such as the Lions or Jaycees. The number of people who avoid any direct engagement in politics or government, such as voting in a national election, has increased. Where people once sought a common public life to which the individual was expected to both concede and agreeably support, the pattern that has emerged in the unraveling is one of private control and personal satisfaction. People bowl, but they do so on their own time and own schedule without conforming to the expectations of group leagues.

This consumer-oriented society in which individuals expect their own needs to be met can also be seen in the work on "privatopia" by

Evan McKenzie, an assistant professor of political science at Albright College. McKenzie tracks the political and social issues created by new forms of housing in America such as condominiums, co-ops, planned-unit developments, and gated communities.[22] Based on a dominant ideology of privatism, participants in these new forms of housing are developing residential, private governments that perform many of the functions of local government, such as police protection, trash collection, and street maintenance, but which also often require behavioral covenants for living together with others. It is as if small collections of people gather together to enforce a controlled and livable environment that has escaped them on a larger social or national level.

The Default of Congregations

In the various shifts of values and behaviors that have been broadly outlined above, we see a notable change in the public relationships among people which allows for, and perhaps encourages, less-than-civil norms. The change provides a supportive environment for a host of aggressive and individualistic behaviors and experiences including road rage, corporate downsizing, resurgent racism, entertainment such as ultimate fighting, and "gotcha" investigative reporting. This culturally sanctioned, aggressive behavior is what author and professor Nicholas Mills calls the "triumph of meanness." He argues that meanness in the 1990s is not just a political response but a state of mind, the product of a culture of spite and cruelty.[23] Writes Mills, "For an increasing percentage of the country, the obligations of nationhood have turned into a burden, and what the culture of meanness has supplied is the justification for those who feel this way to shed their connection with everyone but people like themselves."[24] Clearly, the culture of meanness has intruded into the lives of a number of our congregations.

Whether the term "culture of meanness" is an overstatement or not, there is a spreading recognition that we are experiencing a cultural resurgence of individualism and self-orientation which Stephen Carter, William Nelson Cromwell Professor of Law at Yale, calls an "incivility crisis." Typical, and perhaps symptomatic, of this crisis is the story of the "selfish passenger" that Carter relates about the man who raced past the security gates at the Houston Intercontinental Airport in July of

1995.[25] Probably late for a flight and not willing to be slowed down by going through the metal detectors, the man dashed past guards who were too surprised to react quickly enough. The man disappeared into the crowd. Because they were not sure that the man was unarmed, the airport authorities decided to evacuate both Continental Airlines terminals, requiring over 7,000 persons to leave and go through security screening again before reentering the terminals. The process took over four hours, delayed 40 flights, and caused thousands of passengers to miss connecting flights. What is measured in this example is not an in-your-face, aggressive spirit of meanness, but rather a simple selfishness in which the rushing man thought only of his own need to be on time without counting the cost or harm that he might do to others.

If there are any antidotes to the meanness and selfishness that currently accompany the movements of generations in our society, we would expect to find them in congregations where people follow and share their faith. One would expect congregations to be places where the values and the disciplines of the faith would be both taught and practiced. But, as the examples at the beginning of this chapter suggest, congregations are places where people sometimes continue to practice their incivility rather than claim a position against it.

I often talk with leaders about the fact that congregations seem to have defaulted to the standards and the behaviors of the culture rather than claimed and followed the standards and behaviors of their own faith. I use the word default as it is used with computers. Each of our computer software programs includes certain defaults that are fallback settings which guide the program's behavior. For instance, my word processing program has preset defaults that determine the margins, line spacing, font, and size. I do not have to set these characteristics each time I use the program because they are selected by default. I can, of course, set other standards as new defaults, and that is the key. If I do not set new standards for my software, it will simply default to prior settings. In much the same way, our congregations have defaulted to community or cultural standards of behavior. Remove the "bookend prayers"–the prayers at the beginning and end of the meeting–and many of our congregational or committee meetings would not look significantly different from meetings of other community groups such as the school board, zoning board, or parent teacher association. In all cases, congregations included, one would expect to find hidden agendas, oppositional subgroups, blaming, and in too many cases, accusations and name-calling. Unless congregations change their default system, unless we consciously choose to follow the values and practices of our faith as we live together in community, we will continue to look and behave like most other organizations and communities that are participating in the unraveling of the current culture wars.

While we might believe that we have to accept the political battling that is taking place in the public sector, Stephen Carter notes that there should be other places—our social clubs, our community centers, our college classrooms, and our congregations—where we could go to forget and escape the confrontational and uncivil nature of the day. But Carter concludes with what our experience confirms, that too often these other places have been swayed by the culture.

> But the other spheres of social life are dying—or, if they survive, they are coming to mimic, or even to be engulfed by, the model of political vitriol. The universities, the churches, the public schools, the few remaining social clubs, even the family . . . , all have become battlegrounds of the same political style (and over many of the same issues) that we see in our partisan fights.[26]

Like so many other places in our public lives, our congregations have also walked through the recent generational turnings that have left their impact on our lives. Our congregations easily remember the time of the high when the GI values of management, conformity, stability, and group identity held sway. In many of our congregations these were the foundational lessons of life for many of the people who are still the leaders. People easily remember the days when attendance at worship was higher, when the congregation was the center of social life, when young couples gathered regularly for recreational times, when all of the women participated in circles or volunteer groups, and when all the youth attended the youth group meetings and outings. In a good number of congregations the period of the high is still recalled as "the golden age of King David" to which people wish to return rather than look ahead at what comes next.

Our congregations have also experienced the awakening when whole groups of people challenged the status quo with questions of spirit and statements of ideals. As individuals began to assert themselves independently and began to question their trust in institutions as guideposts or caretakers, a whole segment of a generation chose to stay away from institutions, congregations included. Many of our congregations are missing a generation of people who are now in their mid-forties to early sixties and who, in their individual idealism and searching, have stayed away from congregations.

Just as our congregations have participated in the high and the awakening, so they find themselves as active, if not reluctant, participants in the unraveling. The concern that members of so many congregations feel about their worship and programs being "market-driven" reflects their reaction to the social preference today for institutions to seek and to serve the individual, not the other way around. The excessive complaints and conflicting preferences in congregations reflect the current culture in which every individual assumes that, like Burger King taught us, we are to "have it our way." The tiredness that many leaders experience comes from trying to be all things to all people in a crowded marketplace with multiple demands and expectations. It is no surprise that it is our largest congregations that continue to grow and claim an ever increasing percentage of the total membership of our denominations (even though there are fewer large congregations); it is the largest congregations that have the volunteers, space, dollars, and staff to accommodate all of the differing demands of the individuals who make up the congregation.

If we have so naturally participated in the social and cultural tides that have moved the secular facet of our lives (and who would have expected our congregations or members not to have participated and been influenced?), we should not be surprised or disappointed that our congregations also reflect a measure of the mean spiritedness and the incivility that are so prevalent today. We are responding to the cultural default of social behavior. Should our congregations be more thoughtful about their behavior as a faith community? Yes. Should people in our congregations practice behavioral disciplines both inside and outside the congregation that reflect their faith as much as, or more than, their culture? Yes. But these things will not happen unless the leaders of our congregations intentionally reset the default system for behaviors that reflect their faith.

Is This All Bad News?

At this point, whether I think about you reading this chapter or about my conversations with congregations I am working with, I begin to wonder if this all sounds like bad news to people. I sometimes think that I am looking at people whose eyes have glazed over because they are feeling hopeless. After all, if the whole culture has conspired to be individualistic to the point of selfishness and incivility, can we hope for anything different in our congregations? I image people are saying, "If this is really the way things are going to be, I don't want to sign on as a board member or a chairperson of a committee where people will complain about me and perhaps talk behind my back." I imagine a darkness creeping over the clergy in these conversations who wonder why in the world they responded to a call to ministry at this time in our culture. You know, "Just my luck to be a leader when nobody likes leaders!"

I want, however, to hold my ground and to suggest that the situation I am describing is not bad news. For each of us, every stage of our lives holds its own challenges, and every chapter in our shared history as a people has its own characteristics. The current setting of competing preferences and uncivil behavior is not a problem to be solved as much as a moment to be understood.

These current conditions are not problems to be solved because, in most cases, the solution is beyond our control. Recently, during a visit by our oldest son, we were laughing together about a time when he was in high school. He went through a growth spurt and having suddenly grown by almost two inches, lost his balance and coordination. An excellent soccer player, he suddenly went from easy balance and impressive ball control to not being able to run in a straight line without tripping over his own feet. His coach asked him if he was tripping over the lines that marked the field! Stuck with a body that had suddenly grown beyond his control, he sat at our kitchen table one evening totally exasperated and yelling "Arghhh!" when the bowl of ice cream he was eating suddenly catapulted out of his hands and ended upside down on his knee. Was his rapid growth a problem to be solved? No. Was it something that he could control? No. Was he going to have to learn new things about himself and learn how to be himself in a new way? Definitely.

The setting that many of our congregations and our congregational leaders find themselves in is much like the one our son experienced. The incivility and the individualism of the culture that faces our congregations are not a problem. To consider them a problem leads us to think that we can somehow correct or fix them. The current setting of our culture is out of our immediate control. Congregations that sit behind closed doors and complain about the insensitive, uncaring, and unspiritual people "out there" in the community soon discover that they have isolated themselves from the very place to which they have been called to offer their faith. Living in the midst of an unraveling is not a problem to be solved. It is a condition about which we need to learn new things in order to be people of authentic faith.

There is a very interesting conversation in Ronald Heifetz's book *Leadership Without Easy Answers*, one of the best resources on leadership of which I am aware. Heifetz argues that leaders need to distinguish between situations which require *technical* responses and those which require *adaptive* responses.[27] In technical situations both the defining of the problem and the solution to the problem are clear and understandable. A typical technical situation facing a congregation might involve information from a heating contractor, who explains that the boiler in the original section of the plant is now 75 years old and replacement parts are no longer available. It is a clear problem and the facilities committee will probably move quickly to a clear solution, gathering estimates from contractors on the cost of replacing the boiler before the next heating season.

But adaptive situations are quite different. In adaptive situations, the solution (and sometimes even the problem) is not clear and leaders cannot act or move to a solution until they learn more about the situation and the context in which they are experiencing the problem. An adaptive situation might involve questions about providing religious education to children who are most often sporadic in their attendance. Recalling an earlier time in New England history when families would rent a pew in which they had exclusive rights to sit Sunday after Sunday, one rector jokes that his people no longer rent their pews; they invest in timeshares. They pay to use the pew only on selected Sundays and leave the pew to be used by others on other Sundays. How then does a congregation approach religious teaching with any coherence or consistency when both teacher and student come in and out of "time share" class sessions? While the problem is relatively clear, there is no clear solution. The leaders have to learn more about the lifestyles of their families in order to know how and when to engage the children and families in religious education. They have to learn more about the purpose and function of religious training, and how to share the stories, beliefs, and disciplines of their faith using other methods than the standard classroom models based on a standardized curriculum.

Heifetz addresses the current cultural setting, one of an unraveling and uncivil behavior, when he suggests there are times when leaders need to accept that a problem is not even a problem, that is, that it is not changeable. Some problems stop being problems and simply become the context or the condition under which we will live. Director of the Leadership Education Project at Harvard, Heifetz is also a psychiatrist with medical training, and he uses medical conditions to illustrate his ideas. His examples of fully adaptive situations include chronic illness or impending death. The critical distinction that needs to be understood is that once a patient has been diagnosed with a chronic illness, "solving" the problem is no longer an issue. A chronic illness cannot be solved. In fact, by its diagnosis it is recognized as unsolvable. Because the chronic illness is not a problem to be solved, it instead needs to be understood as a *condition* with which that person will now continue to live. In order to live with the newly understood "condition," both the doctor and the patient will have to do a lot of "learning" about appropriate doses of medication, supportive lifestyle changes, appropriate development and use of support systems, and mental, emotional, and spiritual acceptance of the new setting in life.[28]

Such is the current situation for congregations as faith communities in a cultural setting of individualism that allows and supports selfishness and incivility as an expression of the worth of the person. This is a not a problem to be solved. Congregations and clergy will not get far by either actively working or patiently waiting for people and cultural standards to be different so that we can all go back happily and harmoniously to the golden days of King David.

Rather, this is a time for the leaders and members of congregations to learn and relearn our own faith commitments and the values of our faith traditions. It is a time to learn how our beliefs and values can be translated into behaviors and relationships that are both healthy and reflective of our beliefs. It is a time to learn about what we can control and what we cannot control. And it is a time to learn the difference between participating in the default to cultural behaviors and embracing a covenant to practice new behaviors that are based on our relationship with God.

It may be helpful to remember that there are places of learning and signposts that we can attend to along the way. We need not be overly concerned about the tension that exists between the harmony of the remembered past and the discomfort that we sometimes feel today. Dorothy Bass, in writing about congregations as bearers of tradition, reminds us that "congregations have stood at the crossroads of conservation and change in American religion, facing back to a cherished inheritance and forward through the contexts of the congregants' contemporary lives. And at this crossroads, a characteristic tension prevails."[29] Within that tension between cherished pasts and contemporary realities, a host of healthy congregations practice their faith with one another and with the community in which they live.

We should be encouraged that there are places in our culture, other than congregations, that teach disciplines and appropriate behavior. For instance, it was interesting that back in 1997 when Golden State Warrior player Latrell Sprewell violently assaulted coach P. J. Carlesimo, editorial columnist William Raspberry commented on why such attacks by multimillionaire, self-centered stars were so *rare*![30] Looking at the bigger picture, Raspberry noted, "Athletics have been more successful in teaching some of our unlikeliest youngsters to respect authority, to play by the rules and to complain even of dreadful treatment through the proper channels." We should be encouraged to know that there are places in our culture other than congregations which value and honor sacrifice and compliance to the standards of the group. In another example, the Institute for Noetic Sciences, an organization whose mission is to explore and understand human consciousness, recently announced the recipients of its *eleventh annual* Temple Awards for creative altruism. These awards are presented to significant persons or groups that have worked for the welfare and benefit of others.[31] There are other places in our culture, in addition to congregations, that seek and teach healthy community, such as Scott Peck's Foundation for Community Encouragement.

Quite clearly, congregations are not alone in trying to stand responsibly in contrast to the prevailing winds of the social environment. But congregations and their leaders need to claim their own space and identity in a culture that is currently living in ways that are somewhat incongruent with faith. Congregations need to stand in a countercultural position, claiming values and practicing behaviors not strongly honored in the larger public sphere. This is not a new idea or experience for people of faith. Highly regarded as a commentator on the current experience of North American congregations through his biblical scholarship, Walter Brueggeman looks back into the prophetic literature of the Old Testament to remind us that we have been here before. Writes Brueggeman:

> We need to recognize that such a sense of call in our time is profoundly countercultural, because the primary ideological voices of our time are the voices of autonomy: to do one's own thing, self-actualization, self-assertion, self-fulfillment. The ideology of our time is to propose that one can live an "uncalled life," one not referred to any purpose beyond one's self.[32]

Brueggeman then goes on to point out that this is the same crisis that faced Jeremiah, who in warning his people, needed to stand against their autonomy. Brueggeman offers textual quotes in support:

> For long ago you broke your yoke
>   And burst your bonds;
> and you said, "I will not serve." (Jer. 2:20)

> But they say, "It is no use! We will follow our own plans, and each of us will act according to the stubbornness of our evil will." (Jer. 18:12)

We have been there before. We will be there again if the cyclical pattern of history, as identified by Strauss and Howe, is accurate. But today we simply need to be able to find ourselves in the bigger picture of our cultural reality and to ground ourselves in the practices and behaviors of our faith. The immediate tendency is to personalize difficult moments and ask, "Why have I been treated like this?" During such times we need a perspective large enough to understand the cultural setting and ask instead, "Should faithful people treat anyone like this?"

Notes

1. Edwin H. Friedman, *Generation to Generation: Family Process in Church and Synagogue* (New York: The Guilford Press, 1985), 27.

2. Ibid., 208.

3. Stephen L. Carter, *Civility: Manners, Morals, and the Etiquette of Democracy* (New York: Basic Books, 1998), 13-14.

4. William Strauss and Neil Howe, *Generations: The History of America's Future, 1584 to 2069* (New York: Quill, William Morrow and Co., Inc., 1991).

5. Ibid., 31.

6. William Strauss and Neil Howe, *The Fourth Turning: An American Prophecy* (New York: Broadway Books, 1997), 101-105.

7. Warren Bennis and Burt Nanus, *Leaders: The Strategy for Taking Charge* (New York: Harper and Row, 1985), 21.

8. Strauss and Howe, *Fourth Turning,* 101.

9. Ibid., 102.

10. Daniel Yankelovich, *New Rules: Searching for Self-Fulfillment in a World Turned Upside Down* (New York: Bantam Books, 1981), 7.

11. Ibid., 227.

12. Loren B. Mead, *The Once and Future Church: Reinventing the Congregation for a New Mission Frontier* (Bethesda, Md.: The Alban Institute, 1993).

13. Ibid., 13-14.

14. Ibid., 14.

15. Ibid., 15.

16. James Davison Hunter, *Culture Wars* (New York: Basic Books, 1991), 52.

17. Strauss and Howe, *Fourth Turning,* 191.

18. Ibid., 103.

19. Hunter, *Culture Wars.*

20. Robert D. Putnam, "Bowling Alone: America's Declining Social Capital," *Journal of Democracy* 6, no. 1 (January 1995): 65.

21. Ibid., 67.

22. Evan McKenzie, *Privatopia: Homeowner Associations and the Rise of Residential Private Government* (New Haven: Yale University Press, 1994).

23. Nicolaus Mills, *The Triumph of Meanness: America's War Against Its Better Self* (New York: Houghton Mifflin Company, 1997), 2.

24. Ibid., 7.

25. Carter, *Civility,* 5.

26. Ibid., 129.

27. Ronald A. Heifetz, *Leadership Without Easy Answers* (Cambridge: The Belknap Press, 1994), 73-76.

28. Ibid., 76-83.

29. Dorothy C. Bass, "Congregations and the Bearing of Traditions" in *American Congregations* by James Wind and James W. Lewis (eds.), vol. 2 (Chicago: The University of Chicago Press, 1994), 170.

30. William Raspberry, "The Way They Play on the Mean Streets," *Washington Post* (December 12, 1997): A29.

31. "Temple Awards," *Noetic Sciences Review,* no. 46 (Summer 1998): 31.

32. Walter Brueggeman, *Hopeful Imagination: Prophetic Voices in Exile* (Philadelphia: Fortress Press, 1986), 19.

CHAPTER 2

The Leader's Response

People used to travel in groups. Unless one was wealthy, public travel was done in a coach, a bus, or a train full of strangers. According to Yale professor Stephen Carter, public transportation worked as well as it did, moving people from city to city as they bumped and jostled each other, because people understood their obligation to treat one another with regard as they traveled. "They purchased guides to proper behavior, like *Politeness on Railroads* by Isaac Peebles, and tried to follow its sensible rules: 'Whispering, loud talking, immoderate laughing, and singing should not be indulged by any passenger' was one."[1] Seeing oneself as a part of a group lends itself to group behavior. One modifies his or her behavior to accommodate the needs of the group. It is quite civilized.

Today we travel in automobiles. And, as most urban planners will attest through their concerns about attracting riders to public transportation and their offering special "high occupancy vehicle" lanes reserved for car pools on city access highways, we most often travel alone. Or, surrounded as we are by the metal and glass bodies of our automobiles that are commonly air-conditioned or heated for seasonal seclusion, and accompanied by the music of our radio/cassette/CD player, we at least have the illusion that we are traveling alone. When travel required that we see ourselves as a part of the group, we gave consideration to the group's needs. Now we believe that we travel alone, and we feel free to accommodate only ourselves and perhaps the one other person riding with us. Consider the difference between Peebles' injunction not to talk, laugh, or sing on the railway in such a way as to bother other passengers, and the fairly common experience of disregard for others shown by the lone driver whose car radio or cassette player is so loud that it can be heard half a block away. The cars closest at the stoplight can actually feel the bass beat of the music hammering away with its vibrations. Traveling in groups seems to produce behavior respectful of group members, and the illusion of traveling alone seems to signal that it is appropriate to behave as if only one's own needs and comfort require attention. Traveling alone also leads to competition among individuals in regard to personal needs or preferences. Someone I know very well, who often listens to classical music while driving, admits that when stopped at an intersection next to a car in which the driver is blasting rock music loud enough for the whole world to hear, she has the fantasy (more than once acted upon) of rolling down her own windows and turning her symphonic volume to its maximum in competition. Writes Carter, "If railroad passengers a century ago knew the journey would be impossible unless they considered the comfort of others more important than their own, our spreading illusion has taken us in the other direction."[2]

It seems that our changing corporate or national perception of ourselves in relation to a group has an impact on our behavior. As we increasingly see ourselves as individuals, we seemingly practice civil behavior less and less. Carter defines civility as "the sum of the many sacrifices we are called to make for the sake of living together" and points out that the word *civility* shares with the words "civilized," "civilization," and "city" an Indo-European root meaning "member of the household."[3] Our cultural shift toward individualism with its emphasis on personal autonomy reflects the belief that we live in a household with very few other members about whom we need to be concerned or whom we need to treat with caring behavior.

In fact, civility does seem to be getting squeezed in our time. We are increasingly recognized as the most litigious society on the globe, turning to lawsuits in order to right perceived wrongs even before we consider actual conversation between the aggrieved parties to see if something can be done to resolve the issue. Incivility has been practiced so much in the political arena and respect has been so stretched and worn between Republican and Democratic legislators that a Bipartisan Congressional Retreat was held in March 1997 for members of the House of Representatives with the stated purpose to rebuild civility in their working relationships. School boards and homeowner associations in planned communities are increasingly forced to make decisions in response to confrontation and pressure groups rather than through proactive strategies to address planning and development.

This broad, cultural pattern is also influencing the way congregational leaders and members address and engage one another during times of change, when anxiety has risen. In fact, our congregations have often defaulted to the values and standards of community behavior in which the preference of the individual is assumed to have priority over the needs or the preference of the community. How else can one understand the behavior of the church leader who called a special meeting of the governing board for a day when the minister was scheduled to be out of town at a conference? She told the minister that the agenda for the meeting was a discussion of the plans for an upcoming Christmas celebration. But when the board members arrived, the sole agenda item was this woman's dissatisfaction with the minister and her wish for new clergy leadership.

How else can one understand the arrival of a handful of concerned members at a congregational meeting convened to decide changes in worship times who surprised everyone present with a signed petition in opposition to the proposal? The petition was accompanied by a long list of signatures that included many people who were inactive in the congregation, who had moved out of town or who were the children and relatives of the complainers. Most of the signers would not have known or cared about the changes had they not systematically been contacted by the small opposition group. The petition bearers had worked hard and secretly for several weeks to gather the names of sympathetic and loyal friends so that their preference would prevail. Although traveling alone is really an illusion, as Carter suggests, we nonetheless believe that we have the right and privilege to be the driver and to say what music we will play—and how loudly—on the trip.

As we've told the story so far in the previous chapter, we have only looked at the cultural polarities of group versus individual, or conformity versus autonomy. As our national story suggests, we have moved in the past few decades *from* a cultural time in which people were rewarded for living out of a group identity *to* a cultural time in which people are rewarded for living out of an individual identity. The world of "group" and the world of "individual" are competing domains with different identities, values, and assumptions that lead to very different daily behaviors. These two domains have historically formed a polarity in which one and then the other becomes dominant. Yet in the midst of this cyclical swing between conformity and personal freedom there is a third domain of living that people of faith can claim and to which they belong. And it is to this third domain that we now need to turn our attention as leaders of congregations.

Three Domains of Human Interaction

At a 1995 commencement address at Boston University, university president and philosopher John Silber quoted Lord John Fletcher Moulton, who described not two, but three domains of human interaction:

> Seventy-five years ago . . . Lord Moulton, a noted English judge, spoke on the subject of "Law and Manners." He divided human action into three domains. The first is the domain of law, "where," he said, "our actions are prescribed by laws binding upon us which must be obeyed." At the other extreme is the domain of free choice, "which," he said, "includes all those actions as to which we claim and enjoy complete freedom." And in between, Lord Moulton identified a domain in which our action is not determined by law but in which we are not free to behave in any way we choose. . . .
>
> Lord Moulton considered the area of action lying between law and pure personal preference to be "the domain of obedience to the unenforceable." In this domain, he said, "obedience is the obedience of a man to that which he cannot be forced to obey. He is the enforcer of the law upon himself." This domain between law and free choice he called that of Manners. While it may include moral duty, social responsibility, and proper behavior, it extends beyond them to cover "all cases of doing right where there is no one to make you do it but yourself."[4]

These three domains of life compete with one another for our attention and allegiance. In their competition one domain seeks to minimize the other. A simple graphic of this experience might look something like the following:

THE DOMAIN OF LAW  MANNERS AND OBEDIENCE TO THE UNENFORCEABLE  THE DOMAIN OF FREE CHOICE

It is no wonder that the middle domain—manners and obedience to the unenforceable—is often minimized or recessive while the dominant domains of law and free choice battle with each other publicly in a democracy. In the argument over large social issues, the two dominant forces of law and free choice stretch themselves in order to capture more attention and authority in the battle for control. For instance, in an issue such as abortion some would seek to write new laws in order to legislate correct behavior (the domain of law), while others resist such laws, insisting that a woman's body is under her own control (the domain of free choice). In an issue such as education, some argue for the mandatory wearing of public school uniforms (the domain of law) as a way of providing focus for children's attention on the disciplines of learning, while others argue that the choice of baggy pants, purple hair, or body piercing, or the choice of wearing a jacket and tie (the domain of free choice) supports the development of peer identity and self-worth. Rarely in this ongoing argument between these two dominant domains is the softer voice of manners, or moral behavior, heard. Yet it is this middle area of moral behavior or manners in which Lord Moulton would insist on some behaviors being practiced simply because people are able to discern right from wrong in conduct. It is this softer voice of obedience to the unenforceable which argues that some behaviors are to be practiced and some disciplines followed simply because they are the right thing to do (the moral, the ethical, the civil), even though they are unenforceable. The domain of obedience to the unenforceable is that area of our lives where we act not because we are forced to (the domain of law) and not because we have the freedom not to (the domain of free choice), but because we understand that it is right to do, and so we discipline ourselves to do so. This third domain of manners or moral behavior is a primary area in which congregations live and from which they offer membership to other people who share both their faith and values. As communities that base their lives on shared beliefs and values, congregations can, and should, expect members to practice behaviors of this middle territory as a condition of membership in the faith community.

It is the domain of obedience to the unenforceable, the middle territory between law and free choice, between conformity to the group (the norms or laws of society) and autonomy of the individual, to which congregations can lay claim. In fact, this middle territory is the province of denominations or movements that historically have developed special disciplines of behavior intended to be practiced as daily acts of faith, both among members and within the larger community. This area of life is not minimized when Lord Moulton refers to it as "manners." For Moulton, manners refer not only to being polite in social settings. Manners also have a moral content and include practices or behaviors based on the ability to distinguish between right and wrong. As Carter states, "Perhaps how we treat other people *does* matter; and, if so, then following rules that require us to treat other people with genuine respect surely is morally superior to not following them."[5]

Moral behavior is not necessarily defined by the domain of law, where people follow the rules because the rules are enforced. Many people don't take the risk of parking in a handicapped parking space, not because it will inconvenience handicapped persons if the space is filled, but because there is a law against it and a fine for being caught. Living in the domain of law is necessary to civilized life because it provides order in those areas of living that need to be shared and where we need to accommodate all; however, simply following the laws that are imposed on all people is not necessarily moral. In fact, some laws are of questionable moral character, as can be attested to by examples that once permitted different treatment of persons because of race or gender.

Nor is the domain of free choice necessarily an area of moral life. Individuals are free to assert their own rights and choices even when their choices diminish the choices of others, such as when exercising the right to smoke in nonrestricted places, even though doing so has negative health effects on nonsmokers.

It is in the domain of obedience to the unenforceable, the realm of manners, that faith communities can claim a special space to practice behaviors that conform to and evidence their beliefs and values about what is moral. It is the area of life in which we are required to behave in certain prescribed ways, but *not* because the behavior is required by law and a failure to comply will be punished. It is also the area of life in which we are not free to disregard certain prescribed ways simply because we can exercise our personal preferences. The domain of obedience to the unenforceable is the area of our lives of faith in which we submit to certain ways of living because we hold membership in a faith community that rests on beliefs and values that prescribe such behaviors. Simply speaking, this is the area of life in which we do certain things because we understand that, according to our faith, they are *right to do*. Moral and mannered behavior is the responsibility of the civilized person. Moral and mannered behavior is the responsibility of the moral person. And in the case of the congregation, moral and mannered behavior among its members is certainly the responsibility of the person of faith. As Carter states, ". . . the freedom that humans possess is not the freedom to do what we like, but the freedom to do what is right."[6]

It is here that congregations possess so many lessons of our faith traditions which are meant to guide the behaviors of our members. The teachings of our faith traditions are a part of the unenforceable domain because they are not public laws that can be enforced. And yet, because of our membership in the faith community, we are not free to disregard them. Unlike laws or rigid rules that, once broken, will result in punishment, the manners of faith are to be found in covenants or promises to practice behaviors grounded in the teachings of the congregation.

For example, Peter asked Jesus how often he should forgive another person who has sinned against him and the answer was, "Not seven times, but, I tell you, seventy-seven times" (Matt. 18:22). In our congregations and in our community life, we are not required by law or by denominational rules to forgive without end. (Seventy-seven times, however, seems to be a number sufficiently large for us to lose count of the number of times we forgive, suggesting that our forgiveness should be without end.) But neither are we free *not* to forgive others. Learning how to forgive and to risk practicing forgiveness are behaviors that should be grounded in the faith community and belong to the domain of obedience to the unenforceable. We are to do it simply because it is right to do.

For example, the injunction of the Golden Rule in the Old Testament to "love your neighbor as yourself" (Lev. 19:18) and the New Testament counterpart that "in everything do to others as you would have them do to you" (Matt. 7:12) are not legal statutes. As members of congregations we are not required by law to obey these commands and to love others, but as members of congregations we are also not free to disregard them and behave unlovingly toward others. We love others as we would love ourselves, simply because it is right to do and because it is a discipline of our faith. Loving others is not always an easy discipline to understand or practice. And certainly people of faith do not practice it because it is understood or practiced in the greater community outside of congregations.

In a sermon preached at the Riverside Church in New York City in 1989, senior pastor James A. Forbes Jr. talked of how he and his congregation should respond to the recent and savage "wolf pack" beating of a young woman jogger in Central Park and how he and his congregation should respond to persons with AIDS who are regularly excluded from full community care and consideration. He said that as he wondered what the appropriate response should be, "a response suggested itself, like a word sent by Federal Express: The church should live by the Golden Rule." He then went on to reflect that he had not heard a sermon on the Golden Rule for a decade or so, adding, "As a matter of fact, I really think that rule is not the current policy of our citizens." But he also observed that the injunction "in everything do to others as you would have them do to you" ends not with a period but with a semicolon. Following the semicolon is the phrase "for this is the law and the prophets," a phrase which, as Forbes explained, ". . . suggests that the Golden Rule is not just some optional extra, added to the Ten Commandments."[7] The behavior and disciplines to be practiced by leaders and members of congregations are moral and they are civil, meaning that they reside in the domain of obedience to the unenforceable. For people of faith the practice of these behaviors and disciplines is expected.

Congregations as faith communities need to be able to depend on the practice of obedience to the unenforceable as a context for the shared faith that binds our members together. We do not have faith nor do we practice the disciplines of our faith alone. We live our faith in the context of community and necessarily see ourselves as a part of a group that shares this faith despite the cultural inclination toward individualism. The values and behaviors of the faith community often stand in contrast to and, at times, stand against the values and behaviors of the culture. Claiming to be different from our culture, we should not accept insensitive, uncaring, or irresponsible behavior in our congregations, even during anxious times of change when differences are most pronounced.

To that extent, congregations need the direction and guidance of their leaders to help them reclaim the midground of the domain of obedience to the unenforceable. Much of the conversation today between the domain of law and the domain of free choice is debate, not dialogue. There is much talking and directing, but little listening or learning.

People are debating competitively and fiercely with one another in order to find ways to win. The controversy between Republicans and Democrats is often uncivil because the two sides do not seek to listen and learn from one another but rather to defeat one another in a struggle for votes representing the power and control to set preferred policies. The wrestling over the ordination of gays and the performance of same-sex union ceremonies has often been uncivil because the polarized sides to the argument have sought to defeat the opposition rather than respond with love to others who experience their faith differently.

These are chaotic times in which differences flourish. In the secular terms of historians such as Strauss and Howe, this is a time of a cyclical turning in which generational values are changing. In spiritual terms it may be more appropriate to say that we are living in a time in which God is doing something new. Again. These chaotic times are somewhat a wilderness experience in which we may feel assured that there is a promised land toward which we can head, but we are not sure of the path by which to get there. For example, it is not always clear what decision to make about abortion or euthanasia because we live in the new territory of a medical science that offers us more control and more options (and therefore more decisions) than ever before. The fact that we have developed a new discipline called biomedical ethics tells us that this is uncharted wilderness in which answers cannot always be clear because questions cannot always be posed in clear ways. Similarly, it is not always clear what decisions to make in our congregations about the way we worship. In many congregations, applauding for our children when they sing in worship will often feel to one generation as an offence to the formality of a tradition that quietly honors the presence of God, while not applauding will feel to another generation like missing an opportunity to affirm that God will accept and love us as we are, apart from traditional formalities and pressure to conform.

The time of the wilderness will always be hard on leaders because it will appear that there are multiple paths that can be followed. And the group or congregation will want clear decisions from the leaders about which is the best path. However, when the time of the wilderness is also a time in which individual autonomy is honored, as it is in our day, each and every potential path that the congregation can take will be championed by individuals who will want to follow it as a matter of personal preference. Some people want to applaud in worship; others do not.

Some people want to sing praise songs in worship; others will insist on well-known, traditional hymns. When the priest, rabbi, or minister preaches, some people will want to be educated and will hear with their minds; others will insist upon being inspired and will listen with their hearts. In the current wilderness, whatever the possible paths, the steps leaders choose to take will be evaluated according to whether or not those steps conform to the preferences of that individual.

A favorite story I often tell in congregations is a Muslim teaching from the Sufi tradition about a judge who was put in the same position as so many leaders (and therefore so many congregations) today. Two men came to the Sufi judge's court with a complaint. The first man spoke to the judge, describing the event that brought them to court. He explained what his neighbor had done in offense, how the consequences had damaged him, and what compensation he expected to receive from his neighbor. The judge listened and when the man was through he exclaimed, "You're right!" Whereupon the second man cried out, "Wait! You can't just listen to his side of the story and pronounce judgement." The judge agreed and so invited the second man to speak. The second man then told of the event from his perspective, what his neighbor had done to him in offense, how the consequences had damaged him, and what compensation he expected to receive from his neighbor. When this man was finished, the judge was convinced again and he exclaimed, "You're right!" "Wait!" cried a third listener in the courtroom. Speaking to the judge he said, "You can't listen to one man and say that he was right and then listen to another who tells the opposite story and also say that he is right." The judge thought for a moment and answered, "You're right!"

As I suggested rather directly in my book on leading change in the congregation, the role of leaders in the congregation is not coming up with the "right" answer and convincing everyone to follow. Too often, as the above examples and our daily experience remind us, there is not one but multiple right answers. The leaders of congregations in today's experience of the cultural wilderness are often faced with no clear answers because we've not been here before, or our leaders are faced with multiple answers based on the preferences or pleasures of the people in the congregation, each no more or less valid than the other, but none of them similar enough to be able to form a consensus. In such a wilderness experience, *the role of the leader requires as much attention to helping the people live together in the wilderness as it does in finding the way out.*

Consider again the use of an Old Testament lens that Walter Brueggeman offers when he compares today's social and cultural dislocation to the experience of the exile following the destruction of the temple in 587 B.C.E. The temple was destroyed, the king exiled, leading citizens were deported, and public life came to an end. There was no group. There was no nation of Israel living intact. The people were in a new wilderness in which individuals and individualism prevailed since there was no center. As the fragmented community responded to the condition of their day, the question facing the Israelites was not "How do we put everything back together and make it right so we can escape this exile?" The hope of returning to a unified Israel was beyond their control. Rather, the question was "How shall we live together while we are in this exile?" Or, stated another way, "What are the appropriate practices and behaviors of a faithful people in this time of change?" Brueggeman suggests that the Old Testament stories and writings from the exile may be one of the few or only resources that congregations today have to move us through the present wilderness and confusion, from chaos to hope.

In the exile some believed that life had been trivialized and emptied of meaning. Displacement of old behaviors, traditions, and practices left people feeling empty and not knowing where to find meaning in the absence of a functioning Jerusalem. In such a wilderness, where there was no clear direction for people to follow or clear behaviors to practice, the appropriate response to the lack of direction for communal life was found in the Book of Leviticus. Writes Brueggeman:

> In response to the crisis of displacement, the Book of Leviticus advocates stringent notions of holiness. We would not wish to follow all these concrete instructions about how to maintain purity and shun defilement. But what is important is that these displaced people, for whom almost everything was out of control, set out to reorder and recover life through an intentional resolve about communion with God.[8]

When there were no shared disciplines of faithful community life, the people reclaimed disciplines that would hold them together with one another and in their relationship with God. Similarly, Brueggeman points to the book of Deuteronomy as a primary document for exiles who have lost the sense of community. "Dislocation," he writes, "carries with it a temptation to be preoccupied with self, to flee the hard task of community formation for the sake of private well-being . . . [in response to which the Deuteronomic tradition] insists that maintaining a public economy of compassion and justice is the way to move beyond despair."[9]

The Old Testament response to dislocation and the temptation to focus on personal autonomy during the exile was the reaffirmation of disciplines and the community practices of civilized and moral behavior—the books of Leviticus and Deuteronomy. As a churchman, Loren Mead talks about our experience with changing paradigms as we leave the Christendom model behind but don't yet know what the emerging paradigms will look like. As historians, William Strauss and Neil Howe talk about the shifting generational seasons and the contemporary turnings of social perceptions of reality. As a market researcher, Daniel Yankelovich talks of the post World War II shift of cultural values from deferred pleasure to instant gratification. Using different disciplines, the observers describe the current exile of dislocation and the present wilderness of personal autonomy in which we and our congregations are living. Our proper response is not to tighten the rules and enforce conformity; it is not yet the season of conformity in our public life. The proper response is not to announce the right steps, path, or solution to get us marching out of the wilderness in a straight line as if there were a shortest distance between our present problems and our future solutions. We have been experiencing cultural complexity and confusion for quite some time. If one or more leaders knew the way out, we all would have lined up and taken the necessary steps long before this.

The proper response of leaders in communities of faith is to hold people steady in their own faith and to ask, "How shall we live together in the wilderness? What promises, covenants, behaviors will we offer to one another and to God while we live, search, and experiment together in this wilderness?" It is futile for leaders to search for problem-fixing answers during a complex and chaotic time. Rather, they must seek ways to live together in the wilderness. The practice of loving, civil behavior in our congregations is a central mark of faithfulness for a community in the midst of any change that comes with exile, wilderness, or just simple differences of opinion.

How Do Leaders Do It?

This is where the "rubber meets the road," as the old tire commercial used to say. It is the difficult task of application or performance. It is one thing to understand that we are in the midst of a cultural shift of values, assumptions, and behaviors. It is one thing to recognize that faith communities have the resources and the requirements to behave with informed care and with uninterrupted love despite the fact that this would require practices significantly different from the culture. It is quite another thing, however, to behave differently as a people of faith who live with one foot in the congregation and another foot in a culture that regularly competes for their attention.

In the present wilderness, clergy and lay leaders alike need to stand side by side and support one another in the practice of "holy manners"—obedience to the unenforceable within the faith community based on shared faith and values—in real and practical ways. They need to remind one another to practice behaviors which clearly announce that rumors and innuendos are not the ways to communicate concerns or disappointments, but that the people of congregations speak openly and face to face about their hopes and disappointments. They need to remind one another to practice behaviors that clearly announce that building a consensus does not mean making everyone happy, nor is it an opportunity for one side to win. People of congregations listen to one another in order to come to agreements that reflect the purpose of their life together. How do we do it? How do we move from an understanding of the current culture, which depends upon assumptions of winning and losing, to agreements and behaviors that allow us to live together in this confusing mix? I would like to suggest three principles for leaders to follow, and then in chapter 3 look at behavioral covenants as a prime strategy to implement change in the congregational default system.

The Principles:

The three principles for leaders to follow are:

- Getting up on the balcony
- Providing a safe environment
- Valuing/managing conflict

Getting Up on the Balcony

This expression is used by Ronald Heifetz to describe our need to distinguish between keeping the whole "game situation" in mind and being swept up in the field of action.[10] As leaders–laity and clergy alike–we are led by our own preferences, experiences, and insights. We are not immune to the emphasis on individualism in our culture. In the midst of issues of change it is difficult for us to see the bigger picture of what is happening to us. Yet, without the bigger picture in mind, it is difficult for us to understand whether or not what we are dealing with is under our control, whether it is important or trivial, whether or not it is our responsibility. In order to escape the limits of dealing with the immediate daily field of action, leaders need to step up onto the "balcony"–the higher, more objective promontory–and help others to see the bigger picture of what is happening. Again, this principle underlines the importance of leaders having some understanding of the cultural descriptions offered in the initial chapters of this book.

For example, a mother of a newborn baby may, in the midst of her sleepless nights and exhausting days, feel resentment and anger toward her new daughter or son. She may blame her child or herself for the mess in a once tidy house, for her irrational feelings of wanting to abandon the baby, or for the changes in her relationship with her spouse or friends that make her feel unwanted and alone. In the midst of the "field of action" of bringing a baby home and beginning new and largely different routines of daily living, it is very difficult for the new mother to keep perspective, to maintain a balanced mind and spirit. However, if the mother of the newborn steps away from the field of action and is able to move into the reflective mode of looking at the situation "from the balcony," she begins to learn about her experience. She might read articles on postpartum depression and talk with mothers who have traveled this route before her. Stepping up on the balcony is taking a look at the bigger picture to see and to understand more than just the immediacy of daily action. The balcony is the place of reflection and learning that allows us to balance and direct appropriate behaviors and performance on the field of action. Learning about postpartum depression helps the new mother to see that her feelings and her experiences fit a larger pattern for which there are remedies she can seek, disciplines she can follow, alternatives she can manage.

Moving from the drama to the balcony, from the field of action to reflection, is often a process of education. The introduction and first two chapters of this book are an effort to move to the balcony by providing leaders a much larger social or cultural context for some of the uncivil behavior that is found in our congregations. Yes, some of the critical and injurious behavior in our congregations does come from mean-spirited and damaging people. There is a field of literature in congregational life that talks about troublesome people and "clergy killers." However, because we often do not have an understanding of the larger cultural picture, it is common for people in congregations to move much too quickly into the mode of blame and to evaluate ourselves or others too harshly when decisions and relationships are handled in a confrontational manner instead of openly and with care. Rather than starting from a position of blaming—accusing people who are difficult in our congregations of being mean-spirited, troubled, or pathological—we need to start from a position which recognizes that people are often doing the best that they can, and that they are using their cultural life lessons in ways that they have been taught are appropriate. The reflective mode of moving to the balcony helps to put the behaviors of people in our congregations into a more helpful perspective. While it is not appropriate in our congregations for individuals or subgroups to push for their preferences in ways that defeat and exclude others, it is important to know that people will often feel free to do so because our current cultural values support and reward such self-centered and confrontational behavior.

Getting the bigger picture by being up in the balcony does not excuse inappropriate behavior or minimize its destructiveness. It does, however, put the experience of the daily field of action in perspective and allows the leaders of the congregation to talk about their own experiences and their hopes for their congregation without always personalizing through blame or self-deprecation.

The introduction and first two chapters of this book reflected on the larger patterns of the culture, or the culture as viewed from the balcony. This reflection will be intriguing and interesting to some leaders in congregations (and necessary for the key leaders of congregations), but it will be an overload and too academic for others. Some may see such explanations as an exercise in offering answers to questions that they are not asking—a strategy that usually has minimal results, as we know from practicing it with our adolescent children as they are growing up. For

those who prefer, there are also other, less formal ways of inviting our
congregational leaders up onto the reflective balcony. For example,
leaders may want to try a brief exercise that invites people to talk about
what is different, and what they hope would be different, between behaviors at their congregational board meetings and behaviors they find
at other business or community meetings that they attend and participate
in outside of their congregation. This might be done by asking people to
brainstorm two questions and write the answers on newsprint or on a
blackboard: 1) What is different between behaviors at our congregational meetings and behaviors at other business or community meetings?
2) What would we hope would be different? Encourage participants to
be honestly descriptive in developing their lists and then discuss the
lists. Helping people to move into a reflective mode by seeing larger
patterns is a fundamental step toward claiming the values and behaviors
they would choose to practice, understanding the alternatives that they
have, and escaping the immediacy of the action that all too often leads
to blame and inappropriate behavior in the congregation. In whatever
way possible, it is important for leaders to get themselves up to a place
where they can view the horizon and gain perspective on uncivil behavior in the faith community.

Providing a Safe Environment

Getting up on the balcony is important for understanding the context for
daily experience. Providing a safe environment in which to talk about
the behaviors practiced in congregations is the second principle for leaders to address. Organizational consultant Judy Brown writes:

> Learning or shifts in thinking, even in the most challenging of cir-
> cumstances, are more likely if we perceive trustable structure and
> authenticity of relationship. That's why many learning experiences
> are marked by a learning structure that is solid and clear (and per-
> haps unusual or non-habitual), and a guide, teacher, or learning
> partner who is authentic and connects with us.[11]

A safe environment is one in which people feel that the anxiety is
managed and controlled sufficiently for them to participate in working

on ideas or behaviors that may have previously been out of bounds for them. A safe environment is one in which they can speak openly, with freedom and without fear of reprisal.

A part of the development of a safe environment is the establishment of healthy *norms* for the group to work by. Norms are the informal and often hidden rules about behavior that control how people will behave in groups.[12] Every group has an established set of operational norms, whether participants are aware of them or not. A safe environment is one in which people are aware of the norms of the group, see them as supportive and helpful to the process they are responsible for, and are able to talk about them.

If the members of the congregation say that they operate democratically and trust the decision making of their elected leaders but, in fact, defer to the two or three most powerful people in the congregation, the environment is not a safe one. If the members of the board say that they enjoy a healthy give-and-take in their decision making but, in fact, every vote is expected to be unanimous, it is not safe to have a differing opinion in such an environment. Groups and congregations need a set of guiding rules that help them to be honest about their actual behavior and to discipline themselves to practice those behaviors. Leaders need a set of norms that allows them to risk exercising their leadership, and members need a set of norms that help to direct the way in which they will respond to their leaders.

For example, leaders need to know that they can speak openly in a meeting without being quoted out of context by other board members. A stated norm of confidentiality needs to be understood and accepted for leaders to feel that they are in a safe environment and that it is all right to talk. Or, for example, board members need to know that once a decision is made by the board, all board members will support the decision in public, even if they opposed it in the board meeting. In order for board members to speak freely and to risk decision making that will not always please every constituency in a congregation, they need to know that they will not be undercut in the congregation by fellow or sister board members after the meeting is over.

It is the responsibility of the key members of the congregation to help set and maintain healthy, guiding norms for living in the community. Setting such healthy guidelines requires that leaders take the time and effort to surface the norms by which the leaders and members of the congregation live so that people can know what is expected of them. When the norms by which the congregation lives are less than helpful or healthy, it is the responsibility of leaders to set new directions and help people to practice more helpful behaviors.

A part of providing a safe environment is providing the necessary time and space for people to step up onto the balcony and learn new insights and risk expressing new ideas. Changing the physical environment for a group trying to understand itself is often an important supportive strategy, for when we return to a particular space that we have used repeatedly for one purpose, the participants will conform to the behavior that they have continuously practiced there. If you want to encourage your governing board to explore ideas and to learn new ways to think about their congregation, it is often helpful *not* to do this in the room where they have regular meetings. The board members have learned that the boardroom is the place where they follow an agenda, make decisions, and often defer to the most senior or powerful individuals in the group. In that space it will be very hard for board members to let go of old operational norms and have a freewheeling, small-group discussion about the way they understand their congregation. Coming away from such a meeting without making any decisions (as insightful as the conversation might have been) will feel disappointing to the board members who are used to making decisions in that space.

A favorite example of the power of dealing with the impact of space comes from a friend who was serving as an interim pastor in a congregation that had a reputation for uncivil behavior and in which a few long-term members dominated conversation and decision making. In fact, my friend quickly discovered that at every meeting in the boardroom, when he sat at the head of the table next to the secretary, the three "power people" sat at the table to his right, while an additional nine board members clustered and crowded around the table to his left. The meetings were often hostile with the power people doing most of the talking, the quiet cluster of nine often talking among themselves, with occasional angry salvos being aimed across the table at the opposing group. Stating that he wanted to rotate the board meetings throughout different sections of the church building "to be sure that board members were familiar with the space that they often talked about," my friend led a migration of the board meetings to different locations in the building. The board members often sat in circles, and sometimes the smallness of the space required that the subgroups of three and nine had to sit tightly together. Using different space changed assumed behavior and helped to change dramatically the conversations of the governing board. My friend noted curiously that it was not until the board moved back into their board-room that they subdivided again and reverted to angry, shouting behavior. It was helpful for this board to reflect on the differences it experienced in its own behavior and performance as it wandered through its own building.

Space provides a context for our conversations, and new spaces often permit, encourage, and bring safety to new kinds of conversations. The use of retreats at conference centers or in the facilities of a neighboring church often helps to coax leaders and members out of their assumed roles, norms, and behaviors in order to think new thoughts and to consider new options. A new, safe environment tells participants that it is not only all right, but expected, that they will think and talk differently in this special setting.

The final key to providing a safe environment is to provide trusted, authentic leadership for settings in which people are asked to get up on the balcony to learn new things about themselves or their congregation. Conversations that are led by well-known and highly trusted leaders feel safe and encourage sharing. Trusted leadership provides a sense that it is okay to talk about whatever our experience or ideas have been. The group assumes that if there is an offense given to anyone, or if a participant begins to act judgmentally or inappropriately, the leader will step in and provide appropriate boundaries so that no one will get hurt.

Often the minister, priest, or rabbi holds the kind of position of trust and authenticity that provides safety for people to participate in conversations of learning on the balcony. However, if the clergy or other key leaders in the congregation have become identified with the discomfort that the congregation has experienced, or when they are identified as part of the cause of a problem, it is important for the congregation or board to turn outside of itself and invite neutral, trusted, and skilled leadership to step in and help them through learning conversations. Congregations can turn to area denominational executives to play this temporary leadership role, or they might invite a neighboring clergy, consultant, or trained individual to step in.

Valuing Conflict

"Criticism is the beginning of dialogue, and, in a vibrant democracy, dialogue is what citizens do."[13] So writes Stephen Carter as he recognizes that civility does not mean a deadening politeness or a denial of differences. While it is our similarities that make us comfortable with one another, it is our differences that energize, stretch, and help us to grow.

Rather than steering us clear of all conflict, leaders need to help people to view reasonable levels of differences and dissonance as the creatively holy places where God brings change. My operational definition of conflict, which I use when consulting with congregations, is simply "two or more ideas in the same place at the same time." Conflict does not have to be a fight. It does not have to be destructive. In fact, consider the reverse. Consider how damaging and destructive (and void of energy and purpose) the environment of a congregation is if it can only hold one idea at a time. This is the problem that many long-established congregations have as they slip over the line of honoring traditions to be locked into tradition*alism*. For example, one congregation became aware of a substantial increase in the number of young families who brought their children to Sunday School but did not remain for the morning worship service at eleven o'clock, a service that was very traditional and formal and did not feel welcoming to many of these young adults. They did not know or understand the traditions. A second, less formal and less traditional service was begun to welcome these newer members into worship. The leaders soon discovered that young families find it exceedingly difficult to get children up, dressed, and out of the house on a Sunday morning to attend an early worship service. Yet, for leaders of this congregation, eleven o'clock was the only appropriate time for the traditional ("real") worship service. So, despite the fact that many of the older members who attended the traditional service were of an age that did not allow them to sleep past six in the morning, the leaders insisted that the "alternative" service be offered at 8:30 A.M., a time which was inhospitable to the intended younger members and, in fact, more convenient for the older members. The new informal worship service was short-lived, and the congregation soon found that a number of younger families were moving to other neighboring congregations with more hospitable offerings. What if this congregation had been able to hold more than one idea at a time and reasonably talk about and make decisions about the differences they were experiencing?

There was no conflict in this congregation. But that was because they did not allow for any engagement of their differences. They insisted upon the civility of false community in which everyone was assumed to be the same and to hold the same ideas and needs. There was only the rigid adherence to the way things had always been done. A congregation that is only able to hold one idea at a time often finds itself in much deeper trouble and with less health and vitality than a congregation that plays with two, three, or four ideas despite the discomfort and the bumps and bruises that come from wrestling with each other over next steps.

Healthy conflict–the responsible exploring of our differences–is synergistic. It brings energy, creativity, and new alternatives to the congregation where once there was only one idea and one practice that everyone had to follow. But healthy conflict is an opportunity to grow in faith and in person only if differences are valued and if people practice civil and faithful boundaries with one another. And so, in the next chapter we will take a look at one strategy that congregations are using to prepare the way. Behavioral covenants are one approach we can take to practice the holy manners we need in order to live together with our differences.

Notes

1. Stephen L. Carter, *Civility: Manners, Morals, and the Etiquette of Democracy* (New York: Basic Books, 1998), 4.

2. Ibid., 4.

3. Ibid., 11, 15.

4. John Silber, "Obedience to the Unenforceable," *Bostonian* (Summer 1995): 50.

5. Carter, *Civility*, 35.

6. Ibid., 78.

7. James A. Forbes, Jr., "Whatever Happened to the Golden Rule?" in *Envisioning the New City: A Reader on Urban Ministry* by Eleanor Scott Meyers (ed.) (Louisville: Westminster/John Knox Press, 1992), 91.

8. Walter Brueggeman, "Conversations among Exiles," *The Christian Century*, 114 no. 20 (July 2-9, 1997): 631.

9. Ibid.

10. Ronald A. Heifetz and Donald L. Laurie, "The Work of Leadership," *Harvard Business Review* (January-February 1997): 125.

11. Judy Sorum Brown, from a paper used with Alban Institute staff during an all-staff learning day on April 2, 1998.

12. Rodney W. Napier and Matti K. Gershenfeld, *Groups: Theory and Experience* (Boston: Houghton Mifflin Co., 1973), 77-104.

13. Carter, *Civility*, 211.

CHAPTER 3

Behavioral Covenants— Holy Manners for a Faith Community

Congregations can develop tools and agreements that can help them face the problems of uncivil behavior by leaders and members. Effectively facing the problems of uncivil behavior depends upon intentionally changing the cultural default of autonomous individualism that currently influences so much public behavior. Congregations are places and opportunities for people to practice other behaviors that are more caring and more creative. The primary way of changing the cultural default system of self-centeredness is by replacing the cultural default system with a new one.

One of the tools that I use with congregations is a *behavioral covenant*. Our congregations need to accept the fact that there will be differences, preferences, and, at times, difficulties in making decisions and setting directions. Indeed, as pointed out earlier, we are helped when we preserve and work from our differences and preferences, but differences and preferences will put us in uncomfortable positions with one another that we will not always understand. The question facing our congregations is "How will we behave (how will we live together?) when we don't understand each other and when we don't agree?" It is at this point that we need to depend upon a framework of civil behavior and holy manners to get us through. One way of finding faithful civility is by developing and following a behavioral covenant. There are some examples of behavioral covenants in the resource section of this book (items G, H, and I). It may be helpful to take a look at several of these behavioral covenants before they are described further in this chapter.

A behavioral covenant is a written document developed by leaders, agreed to and owned by its creators, and practiced on a daily basis as a spiritual discipline. Practicing the discipline described by the behavioral covenant is an action of faith, since practicing such helpful and healthy behaviors is an acting out of one's stated beliefs and values. It is far deeper and more significant than the manners of politeness. It speaks instead of holy manners—the manners of a faith community.

This document developed by leaders is a *covenant*. It is not a set of rules. Covenants refer to promises. The theological understanding of covenant refers to the promises made by God to humanity as found in scripture. While we currently live in a world of *rules* that are often found in legal or assumed contracts, the language of covenant speaks of *promises*. Promises are vows made with the intention of keeping them. When a legal rule is broken, we seek compensation. We want a wrist to be slapped, a price to be paid. When a covenant is broken we seek understanding and recommitment. We want to know what went wrong. What are we having trouble with? How do we try again?

This document developed by leaders is *behavioral*. It seeks to identify and negotiate changes in our behavior, not in our personalities or our values. One of the primary learnings of conflict management is that some things are negotiable, others are not. Behavior is negotiable; personality is not. I sometimes try to make this point when I am working with groups in conflict by joking that my wife has been trying to change my personality now for about 35 years, and, so far, the work is going badly! While this is intended as a joke, it does provide a typical example of the difference between trying to change personality and trying to change behavior. For instance, I am a highly introverted person. Consistent with the Myers-Briggs definition of introvert, I think before I talk, and when I talk, I usually offer conclusions that are not rich in the details or ideas that got me to my conclusion. When I am not working with groups or teaching, I am generally experienced as a very quiet person. If my wife and family hope to change me into a chatty person who talks about everything that I am thinking, the work will go badly! We do not change someone's personality because it is of their essence, their identity. It is non-negotiable. However, we can negotiate people's behavior. My wife can realistically hope to negotiate some agreements with me and expect that I will comply. For instance, she can ask that I not surprise her with my conclusions. In other words, she can ask me to agree not to surprise her in family gatherings by offering a conclusion that affects her without my having talked with her first. Or she can ask me to tell her as soon as possible when I am upset so that she can trust that, although I am quiet, I am in my normal mode and not holding back anger that might be directed at her.

It is common practice that consultants to congregations are asked to help a group through a difficult time in which part of the hope is that we will be able to change the personality of the person or persons who are experienced as difficult. It is often hoped that we will make clergy more friendly and caring. It is often hoped that we will make board members less critical and nasty. Such spiritual or psychological magic is not possible. In fact, such hopes are the wishes that the discomfort being felt in the congregation or in the board might be quickly fixed by changing a person. It is possible, however, for us to work with all the people involved to find agreements about behaviors that will help them live and work together through the difficult situation which left people feeling that someone has not been caring or that someone has been nasty.

For example, one of my favorite stories is about the board that wanted to change the behavior of one of the long-term members who dominated each and every meeting and tried to persuade others of the correctness of his opinions and preferences. This board member clearly spoke most often and longest at meetings, followed at a close second by the minister who tenaciously argued with him to prevent his domination of the board. Most other board members spoke seldom at meetings, and some not at all. What many in this group hoped for was some intervention that would transform this difficult man into a kinder, gentler board member whom they would be able to cope with. But, as noted, changing a person's personality or his or her deeply held beliefs is not possible. Whether a person can change and whether relationships with that person can be reconciled is not up to us. Speed Leas, a senior consultant with the Alban Institute and one of the best-known conflict management consultants to congregations, notes that when it comes to changing a person, "That is God's work. Our aim, rather, is to help one another to be faithful, to seek to create environments in which the possibilities of reconciliation are increased."[1]

Although it is not possible to change people, it is possible to negotiate behaviors and to covenant to follow more helpful, healthy, and faithful behaviors. To continue the story, it was possible with this difficult board member to get him to agree not to speak a second time at board meetings until everyone else had an opportunity to share ideas and preferences. Since the minister was the second most talkative on the board, he also agreed to the covenant of not speaking a second time until others had shared. And since there were a number of quiet or silent members, they also needed to agree that during meetings they would say what they were thinking and not save their thoughts and comments for safer, more comfortable settings, such as the parking lot after the meeting. Behavioral covenants in faith communities are not meant to sanction individuals or to force changed behavior on the people who annoy us. Rather, they seek behavioral agreements to be shared and practiced by the whole group, or the whole congregation, which will help people live together, in and through their differences.

We Are Not without Examples

Congregations and other institutions that seek to develop and use behavioral covenants are not inventing something new. They are, in fact, reaching back into their own traditions to reclaim and reform disciplines of behavior that were understood to be different from the culture in which they lived, but were expected to be practiced by the members of the congregation or faith community. Let's look at several examples, both historic and contemporary, that have been developed in different settings.

Consider first the honor code at Haverford College, a liberal arts college located outside of Philadelphia and founded in 1833 by the Quakers. There are many colleges that practice honor codes in which students affirm a principle of not cheating on exams. However, Haverford College has been singled out as "going far beyond not cheating on tests. The [Haverford] Code is not simply a longer list of rules but, according to information from Haverford's Internet Web site (www.haverford.edu) 'a philosophy of conduct through honesty, integrity and understanding . . . [that] allows members of a diverse student body to live together, interact and learn more from one another in ways that protect both personal freedom and community standards.'"[2] When accepted to Haverford, students are given a 20-page booklet explaining the code and a card that they must sign agreeing to abide by the code. Each year students receive orientation to the code and each year the code is reviewed, amended, and ratified in a plenary process that involves all members of the college community—students, faculty, and staff.

Haverford College caught my eye as an example because our oldest son, Matthew, is a graduate of that college. I easily recall the behavioral specificity in which people at the college agreed to live together. Matthew would talk about the commitment to go directly to the person with whom you had a difference or a dilemma. If the person was playing music too loudly in the dorm, you were expected to go to the person and talk about the situation, not go to some authority about the noise or not harbor anger at your neighbor for disturbing your study. If you saw someone cheating, you were to go to that person and talk about what you saw and what the student was to do about it. You did not go to authorities to report the cheating, and you did not remain silent since that would make you equally responsible for the cheating. I recall the surprise of a number of parents following an incident in the college's off-campus apartment housing in which one of the students called the local police to complain about a noisy party in a neighboring apartment. The police investigated, broke up the party, but also issued a number of citations for underage drinking. When the dust settled, there were a number of persons held responsible by the college code. The parents were not surprised by the college sanctions given to the people who held the party and to the students involved in the underage drinking. That was expected. What surprised the parents were the sanctions brought against the student who called the police. He had broken the code because he had not directly addressed the other students—members of his own community—about their behavior, but had instead gone first to authorities to solve his problem for him.

If behavioral covenants sound different and perhaps more difficult to live by, they are. They are specifically identified as a code of behavior, as covenants, because they are different from the default position of our culture which allows for accusations against others without speaking to them and which allows for seeking one's own solutions and preferences without listening to the needs and preferences of others. Being a part of a community that commits itself to such covenants makes a difference, whether it is a college or a congregation. A recent graduate of Haverford was quoted as saying, "Knowing everyone else had chosen to live under [the code] started you off on a respectful, trusting level that you don't normally achieve with strangers."[3] Obviously the honor code, which was developed out of the religious heritage of the Quakers, reflects the spiritual and biblical background of their faith even as practiced in a college setting that people understand to be an academic and not a religious community. For most of us, however, there are denominational or institutional equivalents that belong specifically to us and which are meant to be guiding statements or covenants to be followed by all members at all times. A clear example is The Moravian Covenant for Christian Living,[4] which was adopted in its original form by the Moravian Church at Herrnhut, Saxony, in 1727. Most of our denominations and movements have such documents, often buried in our books of polity. The Moravian covenant, however, is offered to all members and all congregations as a separate tool and is "recommended for use in the congregations of the Moravian Church in America, Northern Province and Southern Province." This Moravian covenant includes a clear statement of the beliefs of Moravians and is a teaching tool as well as a behavioral guideline for members. Section II of the covenant speaks specifically about the responsibility and behaviors of members in the local congregation. It is there that one finds covenants to respect authority in which members will "abide by the decisions of the official board"; covenants to support the congregation and other worthy causes according to ability by the use of their time, talents, and financial resources; covenants to settle differences with others "in a Christian manner (Gal. 6:1), amicably, and with mediation, and if at all possible avoid resort to a court of law (Matt. 18:15-17)." The covenant addresses behaviors and expectations of leaders and members in the denomination, in the congregation, in the home, in the community, and in the world.

Covenantal documents such as these are meant to guide whole denominations or movements during all seasons. We also have examples of behavioral documents that are designed to guide whole denominations at particular moments in their history. For example, in 1992 the 204th General Assembly of the Presbyterian Church (U.S.A.) adopted a docu-ment titled "Seeking to Be Faithful Together: Guidelines for Presbyterians During Times of Disagreement" for use by presbyteries and congregations. The document begins in covenantal form stating, "In a spirit of trust and love, we *promise* we will . . ." (emphasis added) and then goes on to identify ten guidelines for people to follow. They are clear and behavioral. For example, in a section of guidelines on giving others a hearing, members promise to state what they think they heard from others and to ask for clarification before responding or speaking themselves. In the section on speaking the truth in love, they promise to focus on ideas and suggestions instead of questioning people's motives or integrity and to resist name-calling or the labeling of others.

If there are such covenantal documents for whole denominations for all times, and covenantal documents for all denominations at special moments of difficulty, there are also examples of such documents for special bodies or groups within our denominations that are responsible for particular tasks. For example, during the United Methodist "Dialogues in Theological Diversity," the 23 individuals who worked on behalf of the whole denomination to seek theological understanding and reconciliation produced a number of documents, including ten "guidelines for civility" for use when discussing theological diversity.[5] These guidelines included examples of explicit behaviors to follow, such as "carefully representing the views of those with whom we are in disagreement" and being careful "in the use of generalizations; where appropriate, offer specific evidence."

If behavioral covenants help to sustain whole communities, such as colleges, and support the difficult working of denominations in all of their diversity, imagine the difference a covenant of behaviors could make in congregations. Imagine a congregation in which leaders develop and practice statements of clear behaviors which reflect their faith and which are healthy ways to work through differences and disagreements. Imagine a congregation in which all members affirm and promise to follow the model that is being set by their leaders.

Developing Behavioral Covenants in the Congregation

As noted, there is a rich tradition, historic and contemporary, of covenants of behaviors that have been developed by national bodies or regional structures. No doubt, many congregations would be able to identify and see themselves in such denominational documents, but denominational documents are still documents created by others who are facing different times and different needs. Congregations can greatly benefit by creating and affirming their own covenants.

There is a sense of ownership of a congregational covenant by the leaders who have had the necessary conversations to identify and make agreements on the behaviors with which they have experienced difficulty. It is one thing to see yourself in a much larger, historic doctrine and to say yes, that is the group, movement, or denomination to which I belong, and that is how we are supposed to behave. It is quite another thing to be able to say that, as members of a particular congregation, we have experienced problems with our behavior or we have not practiced certain healthy and faithful behaviors which we now promise to practice as an act of holy manners. Important in the difference is that leaders have taken the time and opportunity to ask who they are as a faith community, or who they hope to be. They have done their homework in identifying the behavioral barriers that keep them from their goal. They have had the necessary conversations in order to share specific information with each other that will make a difference. Using a model of role renegotiation, John Sherwood from Purdue University and John Scherer from the Leadership Institute of Spokane state that "what building a relationship really means is exchanging sufficient information so that the behaviors of both parties are more or less predictable, and uncertainty is reduced to an acceptable level."[6] Congregations can own and be faithful to their own behavioral covenants with greater strength and focus because the information used to develop the covenants belongs specifically to them and consequently, so does their attachment to practicing the behaviors of the covenant.

While each of our congregations usually belongs to a movement, association, or denomination, each also has its own separate and unique identity. Dorothy Bass was noted earlier as saying that the genius of congregations "lies in their ability to express the particularity of a people." While the Golden Rule can be generalized and states that we are to treat others as we would have others treat us, individual congregations will each have some clearly identified ways in which Golden Rule behaviors need to be practiced in their particular setting because of what they have experienced. For some it may mean not leaving anybody out of the information loop so that no one is surprised by some new information that everyone else seems to have. For others it may mean giving everyone at least 24 hours to make a decision so that no one feels forced to make decisions precipitately. For others it may mean a commitment to pray for each and every member of a committee or board, including those with whom one most disagrees. The particularities of which specific behaviors congregations intuitively know are necessary for them to practice in order to be healthy and faithful forms a very wide spectrum. Congregations need the opportunity to say that when our differences become difficult, there can be specific ways in which we will live together. Individuals need the spiritual opportunity, when experiencing difficult decisions or differences, to practice faithful behaviors with one another.

The next chapter of this book will offer several modules (standardized designs) for working with congregational leaders to develop their own covenants of healthy and faithful behavior. While there are several examples of congregational covenants in the resource section of the book, it is important that leaders discuss their own behaviors and draft covenants relating to them. The modules will offer different ways and settings in which leaders can discuss, identify, and implement covenants that will help them live and work together in times when differences exist.

The Importance of Timing

Behavioral covenants are best developed sooner rather than later. They provide a safe environment and can help people get up on the balcony if they are developed prior to the onset of conflict or prior to making difficult decisions that will engage the differences in the congregation. Conflict has an escalating nature. It begins as a perceived difference or a problem to solve. When dealt with proactively, early stages of conflict become learning moments, but when left unaddressed, conflict often escalates to the point that subgroups within the board or congregation advocate positions and begin to establish win/lose strategies against the opposition.

As I noted in my book *Leading Change in the Congregation*, it is never too late to address issues of appropriate behavior; however, it is much healthier for leaders to agree upon appropriate and respectful behaviors before they need to make decisions about matters that will bring out differences. It is much more difficult to stop in the midst of a confrontation to talk about the way in which people are behaving with one another. For example, if prior to exploring a controversial issue at a board meeting all board members are asked to agree not to speak a second time until everyone has had opportunity to offer a first statement, the request may be perceived as a tool that ensures healthy and inclusive conversation. However, if the same agreement is suggested midway through a tense meeting, those who have been speaking often may feel that this is a measure to control them, and those who have been silent may perceive the new rule as a strategy to get them to take sides. When the prospect of change is on the horizon, it is healthier for leaders to begin exploring agreements and behaviors before engaging the issues in order to help participants deal with their differences. With behavioral and attitudinal agreements in hand, different opinions and needs related to change will be more easily managed with maturity and respect.

Ways To Use Behavioral Covenants

The value of such covenants is not in any *enforcement* of the behaviors. Like any tool of change, the value is in raising the appropriate issues and behaviors to a level of awareness and offering ways to have helpful and safe (non-blaming) conversations about them. Three ways that a tool such as a covenant of leadership can be used for this purpose are:

• Read the covenant in unison at the beginning of a board meeting in order to remind people of the covenant goals that they have accepted for their working life together.

• At the end of a board meeting, spend five minutes in small-group or full-group discussion of the covenant, asking for descriptive responses to questions such as "How are *you* doing with the covenant?" or "How do you think *we* as a board are doing with our covenant?" or "Which of our covenant promises do you think we are struggling with the most?"

• Occasionally use monitoring exercises at the end of board meetings. For example, the covenant promises can be easily translated into self-report scales to invite individual responses or reflections. Using the example of just a few of the covenant promises from one of the covenants in the resource section of this book (item G), the scales might look like the following:

• We promise to respect and care for each other.

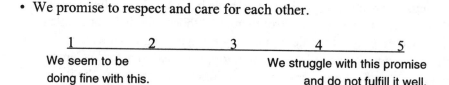

1   2   3   4   5

We seem to be   We struggle with this promise
doing fine with this.   and do not fulfill it well.

• We promise to treat our time on [the board] as an opportunity to make an important gift to our church.

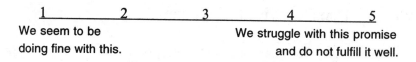

1   2   3   4   5

We seem to be   We struggle with this promise
doing fine with this.   and do not fulfill it well.

• We promise to listen with an open, non-judgmental mind to the words and ideas of the others in our church and on [the board].

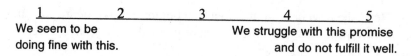

1   2   3   4   5

We seem to be   We struggle with this promise
doing fine with this.   and do not fulfill it well.

• We promise to discuss, debate, and disagree openly in [board] meetings, expressing ourselves as clearly and honestly as possible, so that we are certain that the [board] understands our point of view.

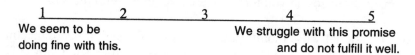

1   2   3   4   5

We seem to be   We struggle with this promise
doing fine with this.   and do not fulfill it well.

Use only ten minutes at the end of a board meeting every quarter to have members anonymously respond to such scales. Ask board members to hand in their responses, then summarize the results on newsprint for all to see. Board members can then easily see if there are some covenantal behaviors that they will need to be more aware of or careful about. Or the results may suggest an item for the agenda of the next board meeting for brief exploration.

Leaders Model Faithful Behaviors—
Mentoring the Congregation

While leaders—clergy and laity alike—have a primary responsibility to manage their own behavior and understanding, they also have a dual and direct responsibility to model and mentor appropriate behavior and learning in the congregation. Changing the way in which a congregation thinks and behaves is not a quick and easy exercise for leaders. It means wrestling with learned behavior which is often practiced without thinking. Learned behavior and practiced assumptions are natural and ingrained, so to invite people to behave or think differently will feel unnatural and uncomfortable for a long period of time.

Changing the feelings and behaviors of a congregation is changing the "culture" of the congregation, for organizational culture is based on the very assumptions of the organization that give it identity and direct the way it will naturally function. As a consultant to organizations that are seeking to implement diversity and to change their culture around very fundamental assumptions and practices about gender and race, R. Roosevelt Thomas Jr. states, "Culture change is a long-term process. It takes years, for example, just to establish supportive traditions."[7] Thomas's reference to taking *years* underscores the need for intentional leadership to help a congregation change its assumptions and behaviors around conflict and differences. It will require leaders who are willing to practice the new ideas and behaviors themselves, and then they will need to educate, invite, and offer an observable model to the members in order to install the necessary changes in the life of the congregation.

Notes

1. Speed Leas, *Moving Your Church Through Conflict* (Bethesda, Md.: The Alban Institute, 1985), 9.

2. Jim Stutzman, ed., "The Haverford College Honor Code," *Conciliation Quarterly* 16 no. 1 (Winter 1997): 8.

3. *Ibid*, 8.

4. *The Moravian Covenant for Christian Living* (formerly known as *The Brotherly Agreement*), available through the Moravian Church Board of Christian Education, Drawer Y, Salem Station, Winston-Salem, NC 27108.

5. *The United Methodist Newscope* 26 no. 9 (February 27, 1998).

6. John J. Sherwood and John J. Scherer, "A Model for Couples: How Two Can Grow Together," *Small Group Behavior*, 6 no. 1 (February 1975): 15.

7. R. Roosevelt Thomas, Jr., *Beyond Race and Gender: Unleashing the Power of Your Total Work Force by Managing Diversity* (New York: AMACOM, 1991), 59.

CHAPTER 4

From Understanding to Action— Modules for Working with Leaders

In this section you will find four alternative strategies for working with leaders to develop and use behavioral covenants in your congregation. These strategies offer basic designs and suggested content to be used by your leaders. The four modules are:

I. Leadership Retreat—One and a Half Days
   (An evening and a morning and afternoon)
II. Leadership Retreat—One Day
   (A morning and afternoon)
III. Board or Committee Meetings
   (20-minute agenda items for use during standing committee meetings)
IV. Learning Team—Four Evening Meetings
   (Working with a team of leaders who meet for the specific task of developing behavioral covenants)

Each of the four modules uses the resource materials that can be found in the resource section of this book, beginning on page 95. The materials in the resource section are reproducible and come with permission to photocopy for use with your congregation.

Each module can stand on its own as a workshop or a process by which to engage leaders in this work; however, the available time or interest of your leaders may suggest that you adapt or combine several of the approaches found here. You are encouraged to read through all four modules and adapt them in ways that seem to be most appropriate to your particular setting and group. Trust your instincts.

Module I

LEADERSHIP RETREAT—ONE AND A HALF DAYS
One evening: 7:00 P.M. to 9:30 P.M.
One day: 9:00 A.M. to 3:00 P.M.

Group Prework

It is helpful if the leader of the retreat introduces the theme and the purpose of the retreat well in advance. This can be done when determining retreat dates or at the time of inviting participants to attend. At least two weeks prior to the retreat photocopy and distribute "Holy Manners: The Spiritual Politeness of Healthy Congregations" (resource section, item A) to all participants and ask them to read this introductory resource as a way of preparing.

If it is a practice of your congregation, invite participants to pray regularly during the week preceding the retreat, for their time together and for their fellow participants who will be with them at the retreat.

Evening Session

1. Gathering (10 to 45 minutes)
    See "Gathering" in Resource B. (If an extended gathering time to make personal introductions is needed, the following components for the evening session will need to be abbreviated.)

2. Prayer (5 minutes)
    Please follow the tradition and custom of your congregation for opening meetings and inviting God's presence with your group and your work.

3. Statement of Purpose and Agenda (5 minutes)
    The leader should offer a brief statement of purpose to remind people of the focus of their work and time together. It is also helpful for the leader to offer a very broad description of how the group will be asked to work (e.g., "Tonight we will begin by talking about the article on holy manners that we have all read before coming.

We will then be reflecting on when we have seen holy manners practiced in our congregation and when we have not used holy manners. We will also be looking at the future to see if we have any items for which we would want to be sure to use holy manners. Tomorrow we will . . ."). Describing the basic steps or path that will be followed during the retreat helps participants to relax. It is helpful to list the basic steps of the agenda on a piece of newsprint (without time estimates) and post it in the room so that participants can follow the direction of their work together.

This is also the appropriate time to be sure that everyone has basic information about the retreat center where you are working, such as location of restrooms and telephones, times for meals, ending time for the evening, and gathering time for the following morning.

4. Norms for Our Work Together (15 minutes)
    Introduce the idea of norms, the informal and usually unspoken rules that groups follow when they work together. Suggest that there are helpful norms and nonhelpful norms that every group uses or experiences at some time. An example of a helpful norm is "Our group expects everyone to share their opinions and ideas openly when we work." An example of a nonhelpful norm is "At times members of our group only share their real opinions and ideas after the meeting when they meet in the hallway or the parking lot with others who already agree with them."

    Suggest that because your group will be talking about themselves and their congregation, there are helpful norms that will support their time together if these norms are observed. In Resource C you will find a beginning list of helpful norms for the group to observe as they work together. Introduce each norm and talk about it briefly in a sentence or two. There are also blank spaces at the end of the list for group members to suggest other norms or ground rules that they think would be helpful for the group to follow. As participants suggest additional norms, add them to the list if there is general agreement in the group.

    It is helpful for the list of group norms to be given as a handout to participants or for the list to be posted as a reminder and reference during the retreat.

5. Full Group: Holy Manners (20 minutes)
    Lead a discussion of the resource "Holy Manners: The Spiritual
    Politeness of Healthy Congregations" (Resource A), which partici-
    pants were asked to read in advance of the retreat. The purpose is to
    invite participants to talk about the general ideas in the resource
    and to talk about the larger social context in preparation for discuss-
    ing their own congregation, which will come later. Questions to
    help focus the discussion may include the following:

    • Where do you observe our communities or nation becoming less
      civil?
    • Where do you run into uncivil or confrontational behavior in
      your work, your community, or your neighborhood?
    • Do you think congregations have a role or responsibility to in-
      troduce manners, or obedience to the unenforceable?

6. Small Groups: Stories of Our Congregation (30 minutes)
    Break the full group into small discussion groups of five to six
    participants to share stories of the manners of their congregation.
    Encourage people to move around the room and form small groups
    with participants whom they know the least. If there are married
    couples in the full group, invite spouses to locate themselves in dif-
    ferent small groups. Continually mixing people for conversations
    will support team-building in your leadership group.
        Assign the task of "telling stories about the manners of our con-
    gregation" by assigning each group to identify the following:

    • Five stories about a time when our congregation was wrestling
      with differences or going through a difficult period, and we
      witnessed the practice of manners in obedience to the unen-
      forceable
    • Five stories about a time when our congregation was wrestling
      with differences or going through a difficult period, and we
      witnessed uncivil, unfaithful, unhealthy, or embarrassing behav-
      ior (Note: Please remind participants that this is not the time for
      people to revisit the conflict or to assign blame for the behav-
      ior.)

7.   Break (15 minutes)

8.   Small Groups: Future Issues That Will Require Holy Manners (20 minutes)
     Ask participants to return to the same small groups that they were in before the break and to identify the issues, questions, problems, or opportunities facing our congregation in the next two to five years that will stir up preferences and differences in our congregation or our leadership and will require obedience to the unenforceable and holy manners. Give each small group a piece of newsprint and a marker and ask them to prepare their list of responses to be shared with the full group.

9.   Full-Group Sharing (30 minutes)
     Invite each group to tape their list of responses to the wall for all to see. Ask each group to share one or two of the stories about the congregation (both positive and negative) that they talked about in their small group prior to the break. Ask them to read through the list of future issues (questions, problems, or opportunities) that they identified in the small groups following the break.
       When all small groups have quickly shared, invite the large group to reflect on the reports. Did people refer to the same or to different stories about the congregation? Did the small groups all center on the same future issues or on different ones?

10. Dismissal for Relaxation and for Evening's Rest

Day Session

1.   Centering (20 minutes)
     Remind the group that they are doing the spiritual work of leaders by caring for the life of their congregation. Begin the day with a time of spiritual centering. You may choose to lead the group in a period of devotions or conduct a centering Bible study as described in Resource C, "Centering Bible Study."

2.   Norm Exercise (45 minutes)

Introduction (5 minutes): Building from last evening's discussion of the norms to be followed by the group for this retreat, remind participants that every congregation lives by both helpful and non-helpful informal rules. The dilemma is that because these norms are hidden or silent (not talked about), we often have little opportunity to change them. The present exercise will help the group to identify and to surface the norms that they currently practice. There are several areas of norms that are helpful for leaders to look at:

- decision making
- information sharing
- conflict
- complaints
- leadership

Distribute the handout "Examples of Unhealthy Congregational Norms" (Resource E) to help participants with ideas of norms that are found in congregations.

Small Groups (20 minutes): Invite participants to work in small groups of three to five people to describe the norms that currently operate in your congregation. Participants can choose which set of norms they would like to work on (i.e., one small group will work on norms for decision making, and another small group will work on norms for information sharing). The work of the small groups may be helped by answering the question "What rules do we have about [their assigned topic]?" Give each small group a piece of newsprint and a marker and ask them to prepare a list of responses to be shared with the full group.

Full Group (20 minutes): Invite each group to tape its list of responses to the wall for all to see. Review each list quickly and ask the full group if there are any norms that they would like to add to the work of the small groups.

3. Individual Work (15 minutes)
    Ask each participant to identify individually and silently the two norms in each of the categories that, if changed, would support their

congregation's efforts to be faithful and healthy. These would be the two most important norms in each of the categories to consider changing in the future. When the participant has identified the two norms in each category, ask him or her to put a check mark on the newsprint next to each of the identified norms, using a marker. Remind people that the limit of check marks in each category is two per person. When each person has completed this task, he or she may take a break.

4. Break (15 minutes)

5. Identifying Places To Start (60 minutes)

    Full Group (20 minutes): Lead a discussion about the need for differences and diversity in congregations. Invite participants to explore the positive aspects of differences and to recall times in the congregation in which new learnings came from working through differences. Using the handout "Healthy versus Unhealthy Conflict Index" (Resource F), discuss the importance of healthy conflict in congregations. Why would a congregation want to make room for healthy conflict in its life, and what practices or beliefs about conflict make this difficult?

    Small Groups (40 minutes): Break the full group into small groups of five to six participants. You may want to keep mixing people into new, small groups to help them get to know each other better. Their task is to *identify and prioritize* the behaviors and norms that, if changed, would enable leaders and members in the congregation to practice healthy and faithful behaviors and practice holy manners. In order to identify and prioritize their list, the small groups can review the following:

    • the stories shared last evening
    • the prioritized norms from the morning work
    • the "Healthy versus Unhealthy Conflict Index" handout

    Give each small group a piece of newsprint and a marker and ask them to prepare their list of responses to be shared with the full group.

6. Full-Group Discussion (25 minutes)
    Invite each small group to share its identified and prioritized list of
    behaviors and norms that it believes should be changed. (You may
    want to remove previously posted, newsprint responses from the
    walls, with the exception of the "Future Issues That Will Require
    Holy Manners" from the previous evening. This will help the group
    not to be overwhelmed by the information they have been develop-
    ing.) Invite the group to make observations about and to discuss the
    lists. Do we have a developing consensus on what we would want to
    change in order to be faithful and healthy? Would our leadership
    group be different, or our congregation be different, if we changed
    these behaviors or norms?

7. Lunch (60 minutes)

8. Introducing Behavioral Covenants (30 minutes)
    A behavioral covenant is a "written document developed by lead-
    ers, agreed to and owned by its creators, and practiced on a daily
    basis as a spiritual discipline" (chapter 3). Introduce behavioral
    covenants to the group using handouts of examples (Resources G,
    H, and I). Using chapter 3 as a source, make the following points:

    • Covenants are promises to follow, not rules prescribing punish-
       ment.
    • Covenants describe behaviors, not personality changes.
    • Covenants are a daily, spiritual practice.
    • Covenants can be used to monitor behaviors of leaders by peri-
       iodically reviewing the covenant.
    • Covenants can be used by leaders to model healthy and faithful
       behavior to others in the congregation and the community.

    The following quotation is from the introduction to this book and
    refers to Kathleen Norris's spiritual memoir *Dakota*. Read this
    section and invite the group to reflect on the difference between
    general intentions of "loving one another" and specific commit-
    ments to agreed disciplines.

    In her spiritual memoir entitled *Dakota,* Kathleen Norris reflects on the difference that she found between a Benedictine monastic community and a Protestant congregation in a small Dakota town. In both cases the people of these two religious communities were confronted with deep disagreements that severely divided them. In her example from the Benedictine community, she told of a group meeting that began and ended with prayer. As the participants talked about the positions that divided them, everyone spoke; everyone heard and gave counsel. The result was an agreement that allowed all of the participants to remain in the community without feeling compromised or defeated.

The example from the small Protestant congregation was quite different. A woman who was a member of that congregation was stunned to learn several days following a difficult woman's group meeting that a former teacher of hers, and a sister member of the congregation, had actively been criticizing her behind her back. Norris noted, referring to the meeting at which the disagreement took place, that it also began and ended with prayer. This time, however, no one had a say, no one was heard, and community was diminished.

In reflecting on the differences Norris writes:

> One thing that distinguishes the monastery from the small town is that the Rule of St. Benedict, read aloud daily and constantly interpreted, provides definition of certain agreed-upon values that make for community. The small-town minister, expected to fill the role of such a rule by reminding people to love one another, is usually less effectual.[1]

9. Identifying the Eyes and Ears for Our Work (10 minutes)
Explain to the group that they will now be invited to talk specifically about writing a behavioral covenant that they will follow in the future as they engage and work through the various issues, questions, problems, and opportunities that they identified last evening (this newsprint list should still be posted for their review).

Note that groups and committees often write very poor documents and that clear statements are best written by one or two individuals working together. The document can then be reviewed and adapted by the larger group. Invite and identify one or two volunteers (the "eyes and ears" of the group) who will listen carefully to the following conversation and take notes that will lead to a first draft of a covenant to be reviewed by the full leadership group at a later time. The "eyes and ears" volunteers are free to participate in the conversation about a behavioral covenant; however, they will take on the added responsibility of drafting results.

10. Identifying Our Critical Covenants (30 to 40 minutes)
    Lead a discussion about the behavioral covenants that leaders in your congregation should practice in the future for the health and faithfulness of your congregation and as a model of holy manners for your members and the community:

    • Write suggested covenant behaviors on newsprint for the full group to review as they are offered.
    • Stress that the covenants are to be positive statements of behaviors that will be followed and not statements of what is wrong from the past.
    • Remind participants that they are focusing on *behaviors*, not on personality characteristics or individual people.

    When a sufficient list of covenants is generated on newsprint for the group to talk about, lead a conversation about prioritizing the most important five to seven behaviors to be practiced in the future and the best way to state the covenant behavior. Invite the "eyes and ears" to ask any clarifying questions they may have.

11. Next Steps (30 minutes)
    Discuss and seek agreement for the next steps to be taken following the retreat, including the following:

    • The "eyes and ears" will draft a behavioral covenant for the leadership group to review at a later meeting; a second or third draft will be developed from those discussions, if necessary.
    • Once the behavioral covenant is accepted, the leaders will formally adopt and commit to practicing the covenant (some groups like the opportunity to sign the covenant as a way of accepting it).
    • We will decide whom we will tell that we have adopted this

covenant and about the work we have done during our retreat.
- We will model the covenant for the whole congregation and invite them to participate in the covenant for the sake of living out holy manners in their families and communities as well as in our congregation.

12. Evaluation and Dismissal (15 minutes)

Module II
Leadership Retreat—One Day
9:00 A.M. to 3:00 P.M.

1. Gathering (10 minutes)
    See "Gathering" in Resource B.

2. Prayer (5 minutes)
    Please follow the tradition and custom of your congregation for
    opening meetings and inviting God's presence with your group and
    your work.

3. Statement of Purpose and Agenda (5 minutes)
    The leader should offer a brief statement of purpose to remind
    people of the focus of their work and time together. It is also help-
    ful for the leader to offer a very broad description of how the group
    will be asked to work (e.g., "Today we will begin by talking about
    the article on holy manners that we have all read before coming.
    We will then be reflecting on when we have seen holy manners
    practiced in our congregation and when we have not used holy man-
    ners. Then we will . . ."). Describing the basic steps or path that will
    be followed during the retreat helps participants to relax. It is help-
    ful to list the basic steps of the agenda on a piece of newsprint (with-
    out time estimates) and post it in the room so that participants can
    follow the direction of their work together.
    This is also the appropriate time to be sure that everyone has
    basic information about the retreat center where you are working,
    such as the location of restrooms and telephones, times for meals,
    and ending time of the day's gathering.

4. Norms for Our Work Together (10 minutes)
    Introduce the idea of norms, the informal and usually unspoken
    rules that groups follow when they work together. Suggest that there
    are helpful norms and nonhelpful norms that every group uses or
    experiences at some time. An example of a helpful norm is, "Our
    group expects everyone to share their opinions and ideas openly

when we work." An example of a nonhelpful norm is "At times members of our group only share their real opinions and ideas after the meeting when they meet in the hallway or the parking lot with others who already agree with them."

Suggest that because your group will be talking about themselves and their congregation, there are helpful norms that will support their time together if these norms are observed. In Resource C you will find a beginning list of helpful norms for the group to observe as they work together. Introduce each norm and talk about it briefly in a sentence or two. There are also blank spaces at the end of the list for group members to suggest other norms or rules that they think would be helpful for the group to follow. As participants suggest additional norms, add them to the list if there is general agreement in the group.

It is helpful for the list of group norms to be given as a handout to participants or for the list to be posted as a reminder and reference during the retreat.

5. Full Group: Holy Manners (20 minutes)
    Lead a discussion of the resource "Holy Manners: The Spiritual Politeness of Healthy Congregations" (Resource A), which participants were asked to read in advance of the retreat. The purpose is to invite participants to talk about the general ideas in the resource and to talk about the larger social context in preparation for discussing their own congregation, which will come later. Questions to help focus the discussion may include the following:

    • Where do you observe our communities or nation becoming less civil?
    • Where do you run into uncivil or confrontational behavior in your work, your community, or your neighborhood?
    • Do you think congregations have a role or responsibility to introduce manners, or obedience to the unenforceable?

6. Small Groups: Stories of Our Congregation (25 minutes)
    Break the full group into small discussion groups of five to six participants to share stories of the manners of their congregation. Encourage people to move around the room and form small groups

with participants whom they know the least. If there are married couples in the full group, invite spouses to locate themselves in different small groups. Continually mixing people for conversations will support team building in your leadership group.

Assign the task of "telling stories about the manners of our congregation" by assigning each group to identify the following:

- Five stories about a time when our congregation was wrestling with differences or going through a difficult period, and we witnessed the practice of manners in obedience to the unenforceable
- Five stories about when our congregation was wrestling with differences or going through a difficult period, and we witnessed uncivil, unfaithful, unhealthy, or embarrassing behavior (Note: Please remind participants that this is not the time for people to revisit the conflict or to assign blame for the behavior.)

7. Break (15 minutes)

8. Norm Exercise (35 minutes)
    Introduction (5 minutes): Building from the earlier discussion of the norms to be followed by the group for this retreat, remind participants that every congregation lives by both helpful and nonhelpful informal rules. The dilemma is that because these norms are hidden or silent (not talked about), we often have little opportunity to change them. The present exercise will help the group to identify and to surface the norms that they currently practice. There are several areas of norms that are helpful for leaders to look at:

- decision making
- information sharing
- conflict
- complaints
- leadership

Distribute the handout "Examples of Unhealthy Congregational Norms" (Resource E) to help participants with ideas of norms that are found in congregations.

Small Groups (15 minutes): Invite participants to work in small groups of three to five people to describe the norms that currently operate in your congregation. Participants can choose which set of norms they would like to work on (i.e., one small group will work on norms for decision making, and another small group will work on norms for information sharing). The work of the small groups may be helped by answering the question "What rules do we have about [their assigned topic]?" Give each small group a piece of newsprint and a marker and ask them to prepare a list of responses to be shared with the full group.

Full Group (15 minutes): Invite each group to tape its list of responses to the wall for all to see. Review each list quickly and ask the full group if there are any norms that they would like to add to the work of the small groups.

9.   Identifying Places to Start (35 minutes)

Full Group (5 minutes): Remind the group about the need for differences and diversity in congregations. Note the positive aspects of differences and recall several times in the congregation in which new learnings came from working through differences. Distribute the handout "Healthy versus Unhealthy Conflict Index" (Resource F) and note the difference between needed, healthy conflict and the destructiveness of unhealthy conflict in congregations.

Small Groups (30 minutes): Break the full group into small groups of five to six participants. You may want to keep mixing people into new, small groups to help them get to know each other. Their task is to *identify and prioritize* the behaviors and norms that, if changed, would enable leaders and members in the congregation to practice healthy and faithful behaviors and practice holy manners. In order to identify and prioritize their list, the small groups can review the following:

*   the stories shared earlier in small group discussion
*   the prioritized norms from the morning work
*   the "Healthy versus Unhealthy Conflict Index" handout

Give each small group a piece of newsprint and a marker and ask
them to prepare their list of prioritized responses to be shared with
the full group.

10. Prioritizing Our Learning (20 minutes)
    Invite each small group to share its identified and prioritized list of
    behaviors and norms that it believes should be changed. Invite the
    group to make observations about and to briefly discuss the lists.
    Then ask participants to identify individually and silently the two
    prioritized behaviors and norms that they believe would be most
    important for leaders to change for the health and faithfulness of the
    congregation in the future. When each participant has identified the
    two most important behaviors or norms to be changed, ask him or
    her to put a check mark on the newsprint next to each choice, using
    a marker. Remind people that the limit of check marks is two per
    person. When each person has completed this task, she or he may
    get ready for lunch.

11. Lunch (60 minutes)

12. Introducing Behavioral Covenants (30 minutes)
    A behavioral covenant is a "written document developed by lead-
    ers, agreed to and owned by its creators, and practiced on a daily
    basis as a spiritual discipline" (chapter 3). Introduce behavioral
    covenants to the group using handouts of examples (Resources G,
    H, and I). Using chapter 3 as a source, make the following points:

    • Covenants are promises to follow, not rules prescribing punish-
      ment.
    • Covenants describe behaviors, not personality changes.
    • Covenants are a daily, spiritual practice.
    • Covenants can be used to monitor behaviors of leaders by peri-
      odically reviewing the covenant.
    • Covenants can be used by leaders to model healthy and faithful
      behavior to others in the congregation and the community.

    The following quotation is from the introduction to this book
    and refers to Kathleen Norris's spiritual memoir *Dakota*. Read this

section and invite the group to reflect on the difference between general intentions of "loving one another" and specific commitments to agreed disciplines.

In her spiritual memoir entitled *Dakota* Kathleen Norris reflects on the difference that she found between a Benedictine monastic community and a Protestant congregation in a small Dakota town. In both cases the people of these two religious communities were confronted with deep disagreements that severely divided them. In her example from the Benedictine community, she told of a group meeting that began and ended with prayer. As the participants talked about the positions that divided them, everyone spoke; everyone heard and gave counsel. The result was an agreement that allowed all of the participants to remain in the community without feeling compromised or defeated.

The example from the small Protestant congregation was quite different. A woman who was a member of that congregation was stunned to learn several days following a difficult woman's group meeting that a former teacher of hers, and a sister member of the congregation, had actively been criticizing her behind her back. Norris noted, referring to the meeting at which the disagreement took place, that it also began and ended with prayer. This time, however, no one had a say, no one was heard, and community was diminished.

In reflecting on the differences Norris writes:

> One thing that distinguishes the monastery from the small town is that the Rule of St. Benedict, read aloud daily and constantly interpreted, provides definition of certain agreed-upon values that make for community. The small-town minister, expected to fill the role of such a rule by reminding people to love one another, is usually less effectual.[1]

13. Identifying the Eyes and Ears for Our Work (10 minutes)
    Explain to the group that they will now be invited to talk specifically about writing a behavioral covenant that they will follow in

the future as they engage and work through the various issues, questions, problems, and opportunities that will face them.

Note that groups and committees often write very poor documents and that clear statements are best written by one or two individuals working together. The document can then be reviewed and adapted by the larger group. Invite and identify one or two volunteers (the "eyes and ears" of the group) who will listen carefully to the following conversation and take notes that will lead to a first draft of a covenant to be reviewed by the full leadership group at a later time. The "eyes and ears" are free to participate in the conversation about a behavioral covenant; however, they will take on the added responsibility of drafting results.

14. Identifying Our Critical Covenants (30 to 40 minutes)
Lead a discussion about the behavioral covenants that leaders in your congregation should practice in the future for the health and faithfulness of your congregation and as a model of holy manners for your members and the community:

  • Write suggested covenant behaviors on newsprint for the full group to review as they are offered.
  • Stress that the covenants are to be positive statements of behaviors that will be followed and not statements of what is wrong from the past.
  • Remind participants that they are focusing on *behaviors*, not personality characteristics or individual persons.

When a sufficient list of covenants is generated on newsprint for the group to talk about, lead a conversation about prioritizing the most important five to seven behaviors to be practiced in the future and the best way to state the covenant behavior. Invite the "eyes and ears" to ask any clarifying questions they may have.

15. Next Steps (30 minutes)
Discuss and seek agreement for the next steps to be taken following the retreat, including the following:

  • The "eyes and ears" will draft a behavioral covenant for the

leadership group to review at a later meeting; a second or third draft will be developed from those discussions, if necessary.
- Once the behavioral covenant is accepted, the leaders will formally adopt and commit to practicing the covenant (some groups like the opportunity to sign the covenant as a way of accepting it).
- We will decide whom we tell that we have adopted this covenant and about the work we have done during our retreat.
- We will model the covenant for the whole congregation and invite them to participate in the covenant for the sake of living out holy manners in their families and communities as well as in our congregation.

16. Evaluation and Dismissal (15 minutes)

Module III

Board or Committee Meetings
Twenty-minute agenda items
for use during standing committee meetings

Prework

At least two weeks prior to the first board or committee meeting during which congregational behaviors are to be discussed, photocopy and distribute "Holy Manners: The Spiritual Politeness of Healthy Congregations" (Resource A) to all board or committee members and ask them to read this introductory resource as a way of preparing.

First Meeting

Lead a discussion of the resource "Holy Manners: The Spiritual Politeness of Healthy Congregations." The purpose of the discussion is to invite participants to talk about the general ideas in the resource and to talk about the larger social context in preparation for discussing their own congregation, which will come later. Questions to help focus the discussion may include the following:

- Where do you observe our communities or nation becoming less civil?
- Where do you run into uncivil or confrontational behavior in your work, your community, or your neighborhood?
- Do you think congregations have a role or responsibility to introduce manners, or obedience to the unenforceable?

Homework: At the conclusion of the discussion ask the members to be prepared at the next meeting to "tell stories about the manners of our congregation." Ask every member to come prepared with the following:

- Two stories about a time when our congregation was wrestling with differences or going through a difficult period, and we witnessed the practice of manners in obedience to the unenforceable

- Two stories about a time when our congregation was wrestling with differences or going through a difficult period, and we witnessed uncivil, unfaithful, unhealthy, or embarrassing behavior

Second Meeting

Invite the board members to share some of the stories that they have brought from the homework assignment following the last meeting. As the group shares the stories, ask what they have learned about how their congregation behaves in times of differences and disagreements. What behaviors have we practiced that help us and are faithful? What behaviors have we practiced that are uncivil, unfaithful, unhealthy, or embarrassing? Invite people to share their learnings as descriptions of what they have observed without attaching people's names to the events. Collect "learning statements" on newsprint.

Homework: Offer a brief explanation of norms that guide the behavior of people and organizations like congregations. Distribute the handout "Examples of Unhealthy Congregational Norms" (Resource E) to offer examples of less-than-helpful norms in five primary areas of leadership. Ask members to be prepared to share their own examples of norms which they believe that they and their congregation practice. (See Module I, Day Session, #2, page 67 for a fuller discussion and suggested areas to explore.)

Third Meeting

Beginning with the homework assignment of the norms that guide your congregation, collect members' examples and put them on newsprint. If time permits, ask people to offer a brief example of a time when they have seen the norm, which they have described, in action during meetings of the committee or in the congregation.

When the list of norms is completed, post the list of "learning statements" from the storytelling of the second meeting next to the new list of norms. Discuss which of the norms or behaviors in the learning statements that leaders would like to change in your congregation for a healthy and faithful future. If time permits, ask members to put a check mark on the newsprint next to the two norms or behaviors that they think are most important to be changed for the future. The check marks are to be tallied in order to identify the most important norms that are to be addressed by behavioral covenants. (People can be invited to place their check marks on the newsprint during a later break in the meeting or at the conclusion of the meeting to save time.)

Fourth Meeting

Introduce behavioral covenants to the group using handouts of examples (Resources G, H, and I). Using chapter 3 as a source, make the following points:

- Covenants are promises to follow, not rules prescribing punishment.
- Covenants describe behaviors, not personality changes.
- Covenants are a daily, spiritual practice.
- Covenants can be used to monitor behaviors of leaders by periodically reviewing the covenant.
- Covenants can be used by leaders to model healthy and faithful behavior to others in the congregation and the community.

The following quotation is from the introduction to this book and refers to Kathleen Norris's spiritual memoir *Dakota.* Read this section and invite the group to reflect on the difference between general intentions of "loving one another" and specific commitments to agreed disciplines.

In her spiritual memoir entitled *Dakota,* Kathleen Norris reflects on the difference that she found between a Benedictine monastic community and a Protestant congregation in a small Dakota town. In both cases the people of these two religious communities were confronted with deep disagreements that severely divided them. In her example from the Benedictine community, she told of a group meeting that began and ended with prayer. As the participants talked about the positions that divided them, everyone spoke;

everyone heard and gave counsel. The result was an agreement that allowed all of the participants to remain in the community without feeling compromised or defeated.

The example from the small Protestant congregation was quite different. A woman who was a member of that congregation was stunned to learn several days following a difficult woman's group meeting that a former teacher of hers, and a sister member of the congregation, had actively been criticizing her behind her back. Norris noted, referring to the meeting at which the disagreement took place, that it also began and ended with prayer. This time, however, no one had a say, no one was heard, and community was diminished.

In reflecting on the differences Norris writes:

> One thing that distinguishes the monastery from the small town is that the Rule of St. Benedict, read aloud daily and constantly interpreted, provides definition of certain agreed-upon values that make for community. The small-town minister, expected to fill the role of such a rule by reminding people to love one another, is usually less effectual.[1]

Homework: Ask members to reflect on the prioritized norms and learning statements from the third meeting and to consider what positive covenant of behavior they would like the leadership and members of their church to practice in the future.

Fifth Meeting

Gather together the suggestions for behavioral covenants from the members and put them on newsprint. When they are collected, lead a brief discussion of what would be different in the board or committee meetings if people actually practiced such behavioral covenants. Ask for one or two volunteers to draft a behavioral covenant statement for your congregation using the information shared. Ask also for time on the next meeting's agenda to review the draft, make changes, and move toward affirming and using the covenant.

Module IV

LEADERSHIP TEAM–FOUR MEETINGS
One-and-a-half-hour meetings

A leadership team is a small group of leaders who are gathered for the specific purpose of developing a behavioral covenant for their congregation. It is assumed that they will function as an ad hoc group, which will not continue to meet once its task is completed. The leadership team may be a smaller subcommittee of the governing board, or it may be a collection of individuals from various groups, boards, and committees from across the congregation, which represents the various voices and interests in the congregation.

If a leadership team does the necessary work to understand the behaviors of the congregation and develop a behavioral covenant, there is an additional responsibility that belongs to this group. The additional responsibility is to educate others about what they are learning and why they are suggesting a behavioral covenant. For this group to develop a behavioral covenant and to recommend its acceptance and use in the congregation will not be understood if others do not also have some idea of the reasons and purpose behind the development of the covenant. Like many ad hoc groups in congregations, this leadership group is called to work and to learn on behalf of others in the congregation; however, if the ad hoc group does not take steps to teach others what they have learned as a prelude to any recommendations that they make, the natural response of the larger congregation or the board that empowered the ad hoc group will be resistance and questioning of the recommendations.

Prework

At least two weeks prior to the first meeting of the leadership team photocopy and distribute "Holy Manners: The Spiritual Politeness of Healthy Congregations" (Resource A) to all participants and ask them to read this introductory resource as a way of preparing.

First Meeting

Introduction (10 minutes): The leader should offer a brief statement of the purpose of this group to remind people of the focus of their work and time together. It is also helpful for the leader to offer an overview of the four meetings so that participants will have a general idea of what is being asked of them. If members of the task force do not know each other well, some time needs to be given to sharing at the beginning of this meeting (see "Gathering" in Resource B).

Discussion (30 minutes): Lead a discussion of the resource "Holy Manners: The Spiritual Politeness of Healthy Congregations" (Resource A), which participants were asked to read in advance of the meeting. The purpose is to invite participants to talk about the general ideas in the resource and to talk about the larger social context in preparation for discussing their own congregation, which will come later. Questions to help focus the discussion may include the following:

- Where do you observe our communities or nation becoming less civil?
- Where do you run into uncivil or confrontational behavior in your work, your community, or your neighborhood?
- Do you think congregations have a role or responsibility to introduce manners, or obedience to the unenforceable?

Stories of Our Congregation (25 minutes): Break the full group into small discussion groups of three to four participants to share stories of the manners of their congregation. Encourage people to form small groups with other participants whom they know the least.

Assign the task of "telling stories about the manners of our congregation" by asking each group to identify the following:

- Five stories about a time when our congregation was wrestling with differences or going through a difficult period, and we witnessed the practice of manners in obedience to the unenforceable
- Five stories about a time when our congregation was wrestling with differences or going through a difficult period, and we witnessed uncivil, unfaithful, unhealthy, or embarrassing behavior

Full-Group Sharing (25 minutes): Lead the group in sharing the stories that they have identified. As the group shares the stories, ask what they have learned about how their congregation behaves in times of differences and disagreements. What behaviors have we practiced that help us and are faithful? What behaviors have we practiced that are uncivil, unfaithful, unhealthy, or embarrassing? Invite people to share their learnings as descriptions of what they have observed, without attaching people's names to the events. Collect "learning statements" on newsprint and save for use in the third meeting.

Second Meeting

Norms Introduction (10 minutes): Introduce the idea of norms as the informal and often silent (unspoken) rules that individuals and organizations live by. Remind participants that every congregation lives by both helpful and nonhelpful informal rules. The dilemma is that because these norms are hidden or silent, we often have little opportunity to change them. The present exercise will help the group to identify and to surface the norms that they currently practice. There are several areas of norms that are helpful for leaders to look at:

- decision making
- information sharing
- conflict
- complaints
- leadership

Distribute the handout "Examples of Unhealthy Congregational Norms" (Resource E) to help participants with ideas of norms that are found in congregations.

Small Groups (30 minutes): Invite participants to work in small groups of three to four people to describe the norms that currently operate in your congregation. The work of the small groups may be helped by answering the question "What rules do we have about [each of the topic areas]?" Give each small group a piece of newsprint and a marker and ask them to prepare a list of responses to be shared with the full group.

Full Group (30 minutes): Invite each group to tape its list of responses to the wall for all to see. Review each list and ask the full group to reflect on where the small groups overlapped in their work and where there were differences. (Save newsprint for use in the third meeting.)

Individual Work (20 minutes): Ask each participant to identify individually and silently the five norms that, if changed, would support their congregation's efforts to be faithful and healthy. These would be the five most important norms to consider changing in the future. When the participant has identified the five norms, ask him or her to put a check mark on the newsprint next to each of the identified norms, using a marker. When each person has completed this task invite a full group conversation to reflect on the pattern of check marks.

Third Meeting

Introducing Behavioral Covenants (20 minutes): A behavioral covenant is a "written document developed by leaders, agreed to and owned by its creators, and practiced on a daily basis as a spiritual discipline" (chapter 3). Introduce behavioral covenants to the group using handouts of examples (Resources G, H, and I). Using chapter 3 as a source, make the following points:

- Covenants are promises to follow, not rules prescribing punishment.
- Covenants describe behaviors, not personality changes.
- Covenants are a daily, spiritual practice.
- Covenants can be used to monitor behaviors of leaders by periodically reviewing the covenant.
- Covenants can be used by leaders to model healthy and faithful behavior to others in the congregation and the community.

The following quotation is from the introduction to this book and refers to Kathleen Norris's spiritual memoir *Dakota*. Read this section and invite the group to reflect on the difference between general intentions of "loving one another" and specific commitments to agreed disciplines.

In her spiritual memoir entitled *Dakota* Kathleen Norris reflects on the difference that she found between a Benedictine monastic community and a Protestant congregation in a small Dakota town. In both cases the people of these two religious communities were confronted with deep disagreements that severely divided them. In her example from the Benedictine community, she told of a group meeting that began and ended with prayer. As the participants talked about the positions that divided them, everyone spoke; everyone heard and gave counsel. The result was an agreement that allowed all of the participants to remain in the community without feeling compromised or defeated.

The example from the small Protestant congregation was quite different. A woman who was a member of that congregation was stunned to learn several days following a difficult woman's group meeting that a former teacher of hers, and a sister member of the congregation, had actively been criticizing her behind her back. Norris noted, referring to the meeting at which the disagreement took place, that it also began and ended with prayer. This time, however, no one had a say, no one was heard, and community was diminished.

In reflecting on the differences Norris writes:

> One thing that distinguishes the monastery from the small town is that the Rule of St. Benedict, read aloud daily and constantly interpreted, provides definition of certain agreed-upon values that make for community. The small-town minister, expected to fill the role of such a rule by reminding people to love one another, is usually less effectual.[1]

Identifying Places To Start

Full Group (20 minutes): Lead a discussion about the need for differences and diversity in congregations. Invite participants to explore the positive aspects of differences and to recall times in the congregation in which new learnings came from working through differences. Using the handout "Healthy versus Unhealthy Conflict Index" (Resource F), discuss the importance of healthy conflict in congregations. Why would a congregation want to make room for healthy conflict in its life, and what practices or beliefs about conflict make this difficult?

Small Groups (30 minutes): Break the full group into small groups of three to four participants. Their task is to *identify and prioritize* the behaviors and norms that, if changed, would enable leaders and members in the congregation to practice healthy and faithful behaviors and practice holy manners. In order to identify and prioritize their list, the small groups can review the following:

- the learning statements from the stories shared in the first meeting
- the prioritized norms from the second meeting
- the "Healthy versus Unhealthy Conflict Index" handout

Give each small group a piece of newsprint and a marker and ask them to prepare their list of responses to be shared with the full group.

Full-Group Discussion (20 minutes): Invite each small group to share its identified and prioritized list of behaviors and norms that it believes should be changed. Invite the group to make observations about and to discuss the lists. Do we have a developing consensus on what we would want to change in order to be faithful and healthy? Would our leadership group be different, or our congregation be different, if we changed these behaviors or norms?

Fourth Meeting

"Eyes and Ears" (15 minutes): Explain to the group that they will now be invited to talk specifically about writing a behavioral covenant which they will suggest that the leaders and members of their congregation follow as they engage and work through the various issues, questions, problems, and opportunities that await them in the future.

Note that groups and committees often write very poor documents and that clear statements are best written by one or two individuals working together. The document can then be reviewed and adapted by the larger group. Invite and identify one or two volunteers (the "eyes and ears" of the group) who will listen carefully to the following conversation and take notes that will lead to a first draft of a covenant to be reviewed by the full leadership group at a later time. The "eyes and ears" are free to participate in the conversation about a behavioral covenant; however, they will take on the added responsibility of drafting results.

Full-Group Discussion (55 minutes): Lead a discussion about the behavioral covenants that leaders in your congregation should practice in the future for the health and faithfulness of your congregation and as a model of holy manners for your members and the community:

- Write suggested covenant behaviors on newsprint for the full group to review as they are offered.
- Stress that the covenants are to be positive statements of behaviors that will be followed and not statements of what is wrong from the past.
- Remind participants that they are focusing on *behaviors*, not on personality characteristics or individual persons.

When a sufficient list of covenants is generated on newsprint for the group to talk about, lead a conversation about prioritizing the most important five to seven behaviors to be practiced in the future and the best way to state the covenant behavior. Invite the "eyes and ears" to ask any clarifying questions they may have.

Next Steps (20 minutes): While the behavioral covenant is still in pre-draft stage, it is important for the leadership team not to proceed further on its own. If the leadership team begins to review drafts of the covenant in order to perfect it, they will find themselves offering "conclusions" rather than insight or guidance to the rest of the congregation. It is at this point that a discussion of "next steps" is important. If the leadership team has been appointed by the governing board, is this the time when the leadership team should meet with the governing board to share what has been learned and to offer a preliminary first draft for the board to begin to work with, perfect, and initiate? Should the leadership team meet with any individuals or groups to educate (share process and learning) before a draft of a covenant is shared? To allow the leadership team to move too far and too fast without others learning from and picking up their work is to risk having only the leadership team invested in the final shaping and commitment to the behavioral covenant.

Notes

1. Kathleen Norris, *Dakota: A Spiritual Geography* (New York: Houghton Mifflin Co., 1993), 115-116.

Resource Section

INTRODUCTION

In this section are a number of resources that can be used in working with leaders in your congregation to develop behavioral covenants. These resources are referenced for your use in chapter 4.

The first resource in this section, "Holy Manners: The Spiritual Politeness of Healthy Congregations," is an abbreviated statement, or an "executive summary," of the initial chapters of this book. It has been designed to be distributed to the leaders whom you hope to engage in conversations about the behaviors in your congregation. As a resource to be read in advance of the activities described in chapter 4, it is meant to encourage your leaders onto the balcony to understand and explore their own congregations in the context of the larger picture.

These resources are reproducible and come with permission to photo-copy for use with your congregation.

Holy Manners:
The Spiritual Politeness
of Healthy Congregations

"Wait! Stop the meeting!" We were about 30 minutes into a meeting of key congregational leaders that had begun without the minister, who was unexplainably absent. But here he was, storming in the door and waving a piece of paper over his head. "Wait! Stop the meeting," he said, "and read this!" He handed me a letter from his lawyer which named one of the trustees of the church who was present at the meeting and instructed that he was no longer to set foot on the minister's parsonage property (owned by the church) and was no longer to make any unsolicited phone calls to the parsonage at any time of the day. The letter identified the next legal steps that would be taken if the named trustee did not comply with the letter.

How is it that a minister turned to the strategy of talking with a problematic parishioner through his lawyer's letter rather than face to face? Yet, this is not an isolated instance of difficult behavior in a congregation. For example, in another congregation the pastor made repeated attempts to deal with an aggrieved member who was working actively to have the pastor removed from leadership. Each time the pastor met that member face to face, however, he was greeted by a smile, pleasantries, and little or no hint of a problem. In another congregation, a governing board asked their consultant to present its report to a full meeting of the congregation. This was done to prevent the personal accusations and name-calling that board members had experienced in the last several congregational meetings. And in yet another, four members of a 14-member governing board held clandestine meetings to which they did not invite the other board members, and during which they planned a strategy for ridding themselves of their clergy leader. Somehow they managed not to feel disloyal to the rest of the board members or to the congregation, which they represented. What sense can one make of a congregational member who sends in hundreds of dollars worth of unwanted magazine subscriptions filled out with the name and address of his or her clergy as an expression of anger with that leader? Beside being illegal, how is this different from the congregational member who won't talk to another member because she's "on the wrong side" of an issue, or the rabbi who won't fulfill a public commitment he made to a capital fund campaign because he didn't receive the salary increment that he felt was his due?

Perhaps most disconcerting is the fact that most readers will not be surprised to know that all of these are real examples from real congregations. Examples of uncivil behavior that fall outside the teachings of the faith are fairly common in the experience of too many congregational leaders—clergy and laity alike. These stories are disconcerting, to be sure, and ill behavior such as this, when encountered in the congregation, often makes members or leaders wonder why they have committed themselves to this faith community and if they should continue that commitment. Frequently, the experiences of uncivil behavior are more subtle or common than the examples above. It is more likely that members will be disturbed by unkind public comments overheard in the congregation; by the spreading of rumors and gossip; by the use of anonymous information to question the decisions or actions of leaders; by the public finger-pointing when something goes wrong; or by the attribution of negative, rather than positive, motives to somebody's actions.

Should our congregations be different from these startling or common examples of uncivil behavior? Should we expect the behavior of members of faith communities to be more responsible, more caring, and more faithful? The answer is definitely yes! In fact, helping our congregations to move toward more responsible and faithful behavior is a responsibility of the leaders in a congregation. Many of the people in our congregations, indeed, in many congregations, have "defaulted" to the behaviors of our culture and need to be called back to behaviors that belong to faith communities. Before we get to that point, however, it is important to understand the larger context in which this less-than-faithful behavior is happening in our congregations. What we experience as uncivil or irresponsible behavior in our congregations often has a history and an origin outside of the congregation. The examples shared at the beginning of the section don't belong just to congregations. Similar things happen in neighborhoods, community meetings, businesses, banks, hospitals, and friendships as well. It is part of a bigger picture.

The Shift from Group to Individual–A Look at Our Culture

People used to travel in groups. Unless one was wealthy, public travel was done in a coach, a bus, or a train full of strangers. According to Yale professor Stephen Carter, public transportation worked as well as it did, moving people from city to city as they bumped and jostled each other, because people understood their obligation to treat one another with regard as they traveled. "They purchased guides to proper behavior, like *Politeness on Railroads* by Isaac Peebles, and tried to follow its sensible rules: 'Whispering, loud talking, immoderate laughing, and singing should not be indulged by any passenger' was one."[1] Seeing oneself as a part of a group lends itself to group behavior. One modifies his or her behavior to accommodate the needs of the group. It is quite civilized.

Today we travel in automobiles. And, as most urban planners will attest through their concerns about attracting riders to public transportation and their offering special "high occupancy vehicle" lanes reserved for car pools on city access highways, we most often travel alone. Or, surrounded as we are by the metal and glass bodies of our automobiles that are commonly air-conditioned or heated for seasonal seclusion, and accompanied by the music of our radio/cassette/CD player, we at least have the illusion that we are traveling alone. When travel required that we see ourselves as a part of the group, we gave consideration to the group's needs. Now we believe that we travel alone, and we feel free to accommodate only ourselves and perhaps the one other person riding with us. Consider the difference between Peebles' injunction not to talk, laugh, or sing on the railway in such a way as to bother other passengers, and the fairly common example of disregard for others shown by the lone driver whose car radio or cassette player is so loud that it can be heard half a block away. The cars closest at the stoplight can actually feel the bass beat of the music hammering away with its vibrations. Traveling in groups seems to produce behavior respectful of group members, and the illusion of traveling alone seems to signal that it is appropriate to behave as if only one's own needs and comfort require attention.

Traveling alone also leads to competition among individuals in regard to personal needs or preferences. Someone I know very well, who often listens to classical music while driving, admits that when stopped at an intersection next to a car in which the driver is blasting rock music loud enough for the whole world to hear, she has the fantasy (more than once acted upon) of rolling down her own windows and turning her symphonic volume to its maximum in competition. Writes Carter, "If railroad passengers a century ago knew the journey would be impossible unless they considered the comfort of others more important than their own, our spreading illusion has taken us in the other direction."[2]

It seems that our changing corporate or national perception of ourselves in relation to a group has an impact on our behavior. As we increasingly see ourselves as individuals, we seemingly practice civil behavior less and less. Carter defines civility as "the sum of the many sacrifices we are called to make for the sake of living together" and points out that the word *civility* shares with the words "civilized," "civilization," and "city" an Indo-European root meaning "member of the household."[3] Our cultural shift toward individualism with its emphasis on personal autonomy reflects the belief that we live in a household with very few other members about whom we need to be concerned or whom we need to treat with caring behavior.

In fact, civility does seem to be getting squeezed in our time. We are increasingly recognized as the most litigious society on the globe, turning to lawsuits in order to right perceived wrongs even before we consider actual conversation between the aggrieved parties to see if something can be done to resolve the issue. Incivility has been practiced so much in the political arena and respect has been so stretched and worn between Republican and Democratic legislators that a Bipartisan Congressional Retreat was held in March 1997 for members of the House of Representatives with the stated purpose to rebuild civility in their working relationships. School boards and homeowner associations in planned communities are increasingly forced to make decisions in response to confrontation and pressure groups rather than through proactive strategies to address planning and development.

This broad, cultural pattern is also influencing the way congregational leaders and members address and engage one another during times of change, when anxiety has risen. In fact, our congregations have often defaulted to the values and standards of community behavior in which the preference of the individual is assumed to have priority over the needs or the preference of the community. How else can one understand the behavior of the church leader who called a special meeting of the governing board for a day when the minister was scheduled to be out of town at a conference? She told the minister that the agenda for the meeting was a discussion of the plans for an upcoming Christmas celebration. But when the board members arrived, the sole agenda item was this woman's dissatisfaction with the minister and her wish for new clergy leadership.

How else can one understand the arrival of a handful of concerned members at a congregational meeting convened to decide changes in worship times who surprised everyone present with a signed petition in opposition to the proposal? The petition was accompanied by a long list of signatures that included many people who were inactive in the congregation, who had moved out of town or who were the children and relatives of the complainers. Most of the signers would not have known or cared about the changes had they not systematically been contacted by the small opposition group. The petition bearers had worked hard and secretly for several weeks to gather the names of sympathetic and loyal friends so that their preference would prevail. Although traveling alone is really an illusion, as Carter suggests, we nonetheless believe that we have the right and privilege to be the driver and to say what music we will play—and how loudly—on the trip.

Congregations Are Meant To Be Different

In communities of faith there is an alternative. As we've told the story so far, we have only looked at the cultural polarities of group versus individual, conformity versus autonomy. As our national story suggests, we have moved in the past few decades *from* a cultural time in which people were rewarded for living out of a group identity and in which conformity and stability were honored. It was a time of sameness. We have moved *to* a cultural time in which people are rewarded for living out of an individual identity in which personal preferences and personal autonomy are honored. It is a time of great difference. The world of "group" and the world of "individual" are competing domains with different identities, values, and assumptions that lead to very different daily behaviors. These two domains have historically formed a polarity in which one and then the other becomes dominant. Yet in the midst of this cyclical swing between conformity and personal freedom, there is a third domain of living that people of faith can claim and to which they belong. And it is to this third domain that we now need to turn our attention as leaders of congregations.

At a 1995 commencement address at Boston University, university president and philosopher John Silber quoted Lord John Fletcher Moulton, who described not two, but three domains of human interaction:

> Seventy-five years ago . . . Lord Moulton, a noted English judge, spoke on the subject of "Law and Manners." He divided human action into three domains. The first is the domain of law, "where," he said, "our actions are prescribed by laws binding upon us which must be obeyed." At the other extreme is the domain of free choice, "which," he said, "includes all those actions as to which we claim and enjoy complete freedom." And in between, Lord Moulton identified a domain in which our action is not determined by law but in which we are not free to behave in any way we choose. . . .
>
> Lord Moulton considered the area of action lying between law and pure personal preference to be "the domain of obedience to the unenforceable." In this domain, he said, "obedience is the obedience of a man to that which he cannot be forced to obey. He is the enforcer of the law upon himself." This domain between law and free choice he called that of Manners. While it may include moral duty, social responsibility, and proper behavior, it extends beyond them to cover "all cases of doing right where there is no one to make you do it but yourself."[4]

These three domains of life compete with one another for our attention and allegiance. In their competition one domain seeks to minimize the other. A simple graphic of this experience might look something like the following:

THE DOMAIN
OF LAW   MANNERS AND
OBEDIENCE TO THE
UNENFORCEABLE   THE DOMAIN
OF FREE CHOICE

It is no wonder that the middle domain—of manners and obedience to the unenforceable—is often minimized or recessive while the dominant domains of law and free choice battle with each other publicly in a democracy. In the argument over large social issues the two dominant forces of law and free choice stretch themselves in order to capture more attention and authority in the battle for control. For instance, in an issue such as abortion some would seek to write new laws in order to legislate correct behavior (the domain of law), while others resist such laws, insisting that a woman's body is under her own control (the domain of free choice). In an issue such as education some argue for the mandatory wearing of public school uniforms (the domain of law) as a way of providing focus for children's attention on the disciplines of learning, while others argue that the choice of baggy pants, purple hair, or body piercing, or the choice of wearing a jacket and tie (the domain of free choice) supports the development of peer identity and self-worth. Rarely in this ongoing argument between these two dominant domains is the softer voice of manners, or moral behavior, heard. Yet, it is this middle area of moral behavior or manners in which Lord Moulton would insist on some behaviors being practiced simply because people are able to discern right from wrong in conduct. It is this softer voice of obedience to the unenforceable which argues that some behaviors are to be practiced and some disciplines followed simply because they are the right thing to do (the moral, the ethical, the civil), even though they are unenforceable. The domain of obedience to the unenforceable is that area of our lives where we act not because we are forced to (the domain of law) and not because we have the freedom not to (the domain of free choice), but because we understand that it is right to do, and so we discipline ourselves to do so. This third domain of manners or moral behavior is a primary area in which congregations live and from which they offer membership to other people who share both their faith and values. As communities that base their lives on shared beliefs and values, congregations can, and should, expect members to practice behaviors of this middle territory as a condition of membership in the faith community.

It is the domain of obedience to the unenforceable, the middle territory between law and free choice, between conformity to the group (the norms or laws of society) and autonomy of the individual, to which congregations can lay claim. In fact, this middle territory is the province of denominations or movements that historically have developed special disciplines of behavior intended to be practiced as daily acts of faith, both among members and within the larger community. This area of life is not minimized when Lord Moulton refers to it as "manners." For Moulton, manners refer not only to being polite in social settings. Manners also have a moral content and include practices or behaviors based on the ability to distinguish between right and wrong. As Carter states, "Perhaps how we treat other people *does* matter; and, if so, then following rules that require us to treat other people with genuine respect surely is morally superior to not following them."[5]

Moral behavior is not necessarily defined by the domain of law, where people follow the rules because the rules are enforced. Many people don't take the risk of parking in a handicapped parking space, not because it will inconvenience handicapped persons if the space is filled, but because there is a law against it and a fine for being caught. Living in the domain of law is necessary to civilized life because it provides order in those areas of living that need to be shared and where we need to accommodate all; however, simply following the laws that are imposed on all people is not necessarily moral. In fact, some laws are of questionable moral character, as can be attested to by examples that once permitted different treatment of persons because of race or gender.

Nor is the domain of free choice necessarily an area of moral life. Individuals are free to assert their own rights and choices even when their choices diminish the choices of others, such as when exercising the right to smoke in nonrestricted places, even though doing so has negative health effects on nonsmokers.

It is in the domain of obedience to the unenforceable, the realm of manners, that faith communities can claim a special space to practice behaviors that conform to and evidence their beliefs and values about what is moral. It is the area of life in which we are required to behave in certain prescribed ways, but *not* because the behavior is required by law and a failure to comply will be punished. It is also the area of life in which we are not free to disregard certain prescribed ways simply because we can exercise our personal preferences. The domain of obedience to the unenforceable is the area of our lives of faith in which we submit to certain ways of living because we hold membership in a faith community that rests on beliefs and values that prescribe such behaviors. Simply speaking, this is the area of life in which we do certain things because we understand, according to our faith, that they are *right to do*.

Moral and mannered behavior is the responsibility of the civilized person. Moral and mannered behavior is the responsibility of the moral person. And in the case of the congregation, moral and mannered behavior among its members is certainly the responsibility of the person of faith. As Carter states, ". . . the freedom that humans possess is not the freedom to do what we like, but the freedom to do what is right."[6]

It is here that congregations possess so many lessons of our faith traditions which are meant to guide the behaviors of our members. The teachings of our faith traditions are a part of the unenforceable domain because they are not public laws that can be enforced. And yet, because of our membership in the faith community, we are not free to disregard them. Unlike laws or rigid rules that, once broken, will result in punishment, the manners of faith are to be found in covenants or promises to practice behaviors grounded in the teachings of the congregation.

For example, Peter asked Jesus how often he should forgive another person who has sinned against him and the answer was, "Not seven times, but, I tell you, seventy-seven times" (Matt. 18:22). In our congregations and in our community life we are not required by law or by denominational rules to forgive without end. (Seventy-seven times, however, seems to be a number sufficiently large for us to lose count of the number of times we forgive, suggesting that our forgiveness should be without end.) But neither are we free *not* to forgive others. Learning how to forgive and to risk practicing forgiveness are behaviors that should be grounded in the faith community and belong to the domain of obedience to the unenforceable. We are to do it simply because it is right to do.

For example, the injunction of the Golden Rule in the Old Testament to "love your neighbor as yourself" (Lev. 19:18) and the New Testament counterpart that "in everything do to others as you would have them do to you" (Matt. 7:12) are not legal statutes. As members of congregations we are not required by law to obey these commands and to love others, but as members of congregations we are also not free to disregard them and behave unlovingly toward others. We love others as we would love ourselves, simply because it is right to do and because it is a discipline of our faith. Loving others is not always an easy discipline to understand or practice. And certainly people of faith do not practice it because it is understood or practiced in the greater community outside of congregations.

Congregations as faith communities need to be able to depend on the practice of obedience to the unenforceable as a context for the shared practice of faith that binds our members together. We do not have faith nor do we practice the disciplines of our faith alone. We live our faith in the context of community and necessarily see ourselves as a part of a group that shares this faith despite the cultural inclination toward individualism. The values and behaviors of the faith community often stand in contrast to and, at times, stand against the values and behaviors of the culture. Claiming to be different from our culture, we should not accept insensitive, uncaring, or irresponsible behavior in our congregations, even during anxious times of change when differences are most pronounced.

Leaders Need To Introduce Civility (Holy Manners) to Their Congregations

To that extent, congregations need the direction and guidance of their leaders to help them reclaim the midground of the domain of obedience to the unenforceable. Much of the conversation today between the domain of law and the domain of free choice is debate, not dialogue. There is much talking and directing, but little listening or learning. People are debating competitively and fiercely with one another in order to find ways to win. The controversy between Republicans and Democrats is often uncivil because the two sides do not seek to listen and learn from one another but rather to defeat one another in a struggle for votes representing the power and control to set preferred policies. The wrestling over the ordination of gays and the performance of same-sex union ceremonies has often been uncivil because the polarized sides to the argument have sought to defeat the opposition rather than respond with love to others who experience their faith differently.

These are chaotic times in which differences flourish. In spiritual terms it may be more appropriate to say that we are living in a time in which God is doing something new. Again. These chaotic times are somewhat a wilderness experience in which we may feel assured that there is a promised land toward which we can head, but we are not sure of the path by which to get there. For example, it is not always clear what decision to make about abortion or euthanasia because we live in the new territory of a medical science that offers us more control and more options (and therefore more decisions) than ever before. The fact that we have developed a new discipline called biomedical ethics tells us that this is uncharted wilderness in which answers cannot always be clear because questions cannot always be posed in clear ways. Similarly, it is not always clear what decisions to make in our congregations about the way we worship. In many congregations, applauding for our children when they sing in worship will often feel to one generation as an offence to the formality of a tradition that quietly honors the presence of God, while not applauding will feel to another generation like missing an opportunity to affirm that God will accept and love us as we are, apart from traditional formalities and pressure to conform.

The time of the wilderness will always be hard on leaders because it will appear that there are multiple paths that can be followed. And the group or congregation will want clear decisions from the leaders about which path is the best. However, when the time of the wilderness is also a time in which individual autonomy is honored, as it is in our day, each and every potential path that the congregation can take will be championed by individuals who will want to follow it as a matter of personal preference. Some people want to applaud in worship; others do not. Some people want to sing praise songs in worship; others will insist on well-known, traditional hymns. When the priest, rabbi, or minister preaches, some people will want to be educated and will hear with their minds; others will insist upon being inspired and will listen with their hearts. In the current wilderness, whatever the possible paths, the steps leaders choose to take will be evaluated by each individual according to whether or not they conform to the preferences of that individual.

The proper response of leaders in communities of faith is to hold people steady in their own faith and to ask, "How shall we live together in the wilderness? What promises, covenants, behaviors will we offer to one another and to God while we live, search, and experiment together in this wilderness?" It is futile for leaders to search for problem-fixing answers during a complex and chaotic time. Rather, they must seek ways to live together in the wilderness. The practice of loving, civil behavior in our congregations is a central mark of faithfulness for a community in the midst of any change that comes with exile, wilderness, or just simple differences of opinion.

How Do Leaders Do It?

This is where the "rubber meets the road," as the old tire commercial used to say. It is the difficult task of application or performance. It is one thing to understand that we are in the midst of a cultural shift of values, assumptions, and behaviors. It is one thing to recognize that faith communities have the resources and the requirements to behave with informed care and with uninterrupted love despite the fact that this would require practices significantly different from the culture. It is quite another thing, however, to behave differently as a people of faith who live with one foot in the congregation and another foot in a culture that regularly competes for their attention.

In the present wilderness, clergy and lay leaders alike need to stand side by side and support one another in the practice of "holy manners"– the obedience to the unenforceable within the faith community based on shared faith and values–in real and practical ways. They need to remind one another to practice behaviors that clearly announce that rumors and innuendo are not the ways to communicate concerns or disappointments, but that the people of congregations speak openly and face to face about their hopes and disappointments. They need to remind one another to practice behaviors which clearly announce that building a consensus does not mean making everyone happy, nor is it an opportunity for one side to win. People of congregations listen to one another in order to come to agreements that reflect the purpose of their life together. Because we live in a time in which incivility can break out at any moment as individuals sense and push for personal preferences, leaders need to step out and lead. Spiritual covenants (behavioral agreements) need to be identified and practiced in congregations so that the domain of holy manners–obedience to the unenforceable–is reclaimed by people of faith. It is a primary task of spiritual leadership, by clergy and laity alike, in congregations.

Notes

1. Stephen L. Carter, *Civility: Manners, Morals, and the Etiquette of Democracy* (New York: Basic Books, 1998), 4.

2. Ibid., 4.

3. Ibid., 11, 15.

4. John Silber, "Obedience to the Unenforceable," *Bostonian* (Summer 1995): 50.

5. Carter, *Civility*, 35.
6. Ibid., 78.

Gathering

One of the primary purposes of a gathering time is to help participants step across the boundaries of time, space, and task in order to be fully present with your group and the work you will do. It is a step toward community and helping people feel included and acknowledged, and therefore ready to participate.

If you are leading your group in a retreat setting, it is helpful to invite people to arrive at least one half hour prior to the announced starting time so that they will have the opportunity to familiarize themselves with the setting, say hello to friends, and have a light snack.

It is also important to invite and encourage each individual participant to say something formally to the full group as you begin your meeting during the gathering stage. People who say something, even the shortest sentence, hear themselves speak, observe the group listen to them, and are better prepared to participate again later in the work of the group. The ice has been broken.

10-minute exercise
(for groups in which participants know each other well)

Invite each group member to offer one sentence to share:

• "What do I bring to our group today?" *or*

• "Who needs our prayers?"

45-minute exercise

(for groups in which participants need to get to know each other better)

Invite group members to take two to three minutes to introduce themselves to the group by answering the following questions:

• "What is one thing that you had to not do, or let go of, in order to participate in this retreat?"

• "What is one thing that you are hoping you will gain from your participation in this retreat?"

• "What is one thing that you think no one else in the group knows about you?"

Guidelines
for Our Work Together

In our work and in our conversations we are guided by norms–unwritten and often unspoken rules. Our family life, our employment, and our time together in our congregation are guided by norms which tell people that there are acceptable and unacceptable ways of doing things. Some norms are very healthy and appropriate and some are less healthy and can be damaging.

For our work together today there are some norms, or guidelines, that can be very helpful and healthy if we follow them. They include the following:

- We will remember that our work here today is a part of our spiritual leadership of our congregation. We will treat this work and one another with respect.

- In our conversations we will focus on *issues* and *behavior*. We will not talk about *people*.

- When talking about events or issues in our congregation, we will seek to use words and sentences that *describe* the situation and seek not to use words and sentences that *evaluate* the situation.

- We will talk about our own experience and understanding by using the word "I" frequently. We will not talk about hearsay and rumor, and we will not use words such as "some people" or "everyone."

- We will share information with the full group appropriately so that everyone has the information that they need, and we will not reserve our comments for after the meeting or to be shared only with people who agree with us.

- _____
_____
_____

- _____
_____
_____

- _____
_____
_____

Centering Bible Study

This exercise has been adapted from an African model of Bible study in which participants seek not to learn more facts about the Bible, but rather to use the Bible to open their own minds and spirits to God. An important assumption of this model is that there are no right or wrong answers to the questions, but that we are simply listening to the answers that are within us. Therefore, there is no need to comment on what others have shared. What we share is simply "put into the circle." The need is to listen, to allow each person to share, and to help one another to hear God's Word.

1. Invite participants to sit in small-group circles of four to five participants.

2. The participants are to listen to the same biblical passage read three times. A different question will be offered before each of the three readings. The participant is simply invited to listen to the biblical passage with the offered question in mind.

3. At the close of the reading, the participant is to reflect on the question in silence, and when ready to speak, to simply offer to the small group his or her response. The time of sharing will continue for approximately five minutes following each reading.

4. At the end of the sharing time following the third reading, the group will observe silence to allow individuals time for prayer or to reflect on what they have heard in this exercise.

Biblical Passage:

The leader will want to choose a biblical passage that is related to the theme of the meeting. An example would be Matthew 18:15-22, since this passage talks about appropriate behavior in a faith community.

The Questions:

For the first reading:
What word, phrase, or image captures your attention and remains with you?

For the second reading:
Where does this passage touch your own life experience at this time?

For the third reading:
What might God be inviting us to do or understand in our work together today?

Examples of Unhealthy Congregational Norms

Norms are the silent, unspoken rules by which we live in congregations and all other social settings, such as work or family. While people do not often talk about these social agreements and may not even be fully aware of them, they guide our behavior—for good or ill. Some norms are helpful and healthy, others are not. Below are a few examples of less-than-helpful norms that have been found in congregations in areas critical to leadership. Do you find any of these norms operating in your congregation? What are the norms that you follow in the five areas below?

Decision Making

- All of our decisions must be unanimous; therefore, we don't say what we really think, nor do we disagree with one another.
- Once a decision is made by our governing board, members of the board are free to tell people in the congregation that they disagree with the decision and didn't vote for it.

Information Sharing

- Only the two or three primary leaders have all the information, and it seems as if decisions are made before we get to the meeting.
- We are expected to vote on important issues in the same meeting in which we receive information about the issues.

Conflict

- We believe conflict is bad so we never tell others when we disagree with them.
- When there is a conflict, we expect our clergy to back down and to apologize to whomever is hurt or angry.

Complaints

- When someone complains, we stop everything to try to figure out a way to make that person happy; therefore, anybody in the congregation has the power to stop us with a complaint.
- People are allowed to complain anonymously in our congregation so that we often know that people are upset, but we don't know who they are.

Leadership

- Only the longest-tenured members are listened to, no matter who is elected to the governing board.
- We expect the clergy to be the one(s) to produce all the new ideas for us to talk about and try.

RESOURCE F

Healthy versus Unhealthy Conflict Index

	HEALTHY	UNHEALTHY
1.	ATTITUDE: Conflict is inevitable; it is a chance to grow.	ATTITUDE: Conflict is wrong or sinful.
2.	PERSONALIZED: Disputants are clearly able to see the difference between the people and the problems and do not mix the two.	PERSONALIZED: Disputants quickly mix people and problems together and assume that by changing or eliminating the people, the problem will be solved.
3.	COMMUNICATION is open, people speak directly to one another, and everyone has the same information.	COMMUNICATION is diminished, with people only speaking to those with whom they already agree. Third parties or letters are used to carry messages.
4.	THE BALANCE SHEET is short. The principals address the issue at hand, not what happened months or years ago.	THE BALANCE SHEET is long. The list of grievances grows and examples are collected. People recall not only what they think was done to them but what was said or done to their friends as well.
5.	THE CHURCH IS INTERACTIVE. There is give and take, an exchange of ideas, and a spirit of cooperation and openness. There is careful listening and thought-out statements.	THE CHURCH IS REACTIVE. It cannot be "touched" without exploding. I write a memo to you and you immediately fire back a nasty letter to me.

	HEALTHY	UNHEALTHY
6.	ACCEPTANCE: Disputants acknowledge the existence of a problem and the need to solve it.	DENIAL: Disputants tend to ignore the real problems and deny what is going on.
7.	TIMELINESS: Resolution takes as much time as needed. The parties take the time to go through the journey together, to experience the pain, and to come out together on the other side.	LACK OF TIME: There is a strong need to solve the problems too quickly. People are very solution-oriented and seek to avoid the pain of conflict by saying, "Let's get it over with."

Adapted from *Mediation: The Book* by Sam Leonard.[1]

Note

1. Sam Leonard, *Mediation: The Book–A Step-by-Step Guide for Dispute Resolvers* (Louisville: Evanston Publishing, Inc., 1994).

Behavioral Covenant Example—For a Governing Board

A COVENANT OF LEADERSHIP

Our Promises to God

We promise to pray, alone and together, to thank God and to ask for God's help in our lives and in our work for our Church, and we promise to listen to God's answer to us.

Our Promises to Our Church Family

We promise to demonstrate our leadership and commitment to our Church by our example.

We promise to support our Church pastors and staff so that their efforts can be most productive.

We promise to try to discover what is best for our Church as a whole, not what may be best for us or for some small group in the Church.

Our Promises to Each Other on [the Governing Board]

We promise to respect and care for each other.

We promise to treat our time on [the Board] as an opportunity to make an important gift to our Church.

We promise to listen with an open, nonjudgmental mind to the words and ideas of the others in our Church and on [the Board.]

We promise to discuss, debate, and disagree openly in [Board] meetings, expressing ourselves as clearly and honestly as possible, so that we are certain that the [Board] understands our point of view.

We promise to support the final decision of [the Board], whether it reflects our view or not.

Behavioral Covenant Example– For a Congregation during a Time of Trouble

COVENANT OF CHRISTIAN KOINONIA

Daily Scripture Reading, Prayer, and Reflection with a Special Focus on

- God as one who lives to bring

  New life where we thought none possible
  Hope in the midst of despair and disappointment
  Growth, even through difficult times

- Praying for the pastor and leaders of our church as they devote themselves to serving God and modeling to our congregation what it means to be a community of love, peace, and reconciliation

- Helpful Scripture (especially these letters to churches!)

  I Corinthians (especially chapters 12-13)
  Philemon
  Philippians
  Matthew 18 (especially 15-20)

Christian Behavior, One with Another

- Live by the Golden Rule–Do unto others as you would have them do unto you.

- Do not gossip or be loose with the tongue.

- Invest energy always in ascribing to others the best possible intentions and motivations, *not* the worst.

Summing it all up, friends, I'd say you'll do best by filling your minds with things that are true, noble, reputable, authentic, compelling, gracious–the best not the worst, the beautiful not the ugly, things to praise not things to curse. Put into practice what you learned from me, Paul, what you saw, heard, realized. Do that and the God who makes everything work together will work you into his most excellent harmonies.

> Philippians 4: 8-10
> *The Message:*
> *A Paraphrase of the New Testament*
> by Eugene Peterson[1]

Note

1. Eugene Peterson, *The Message: A Paraphrase of the New Testament* (Colorado Springs: Nav Press, 1993).

Behavioral Covenant Example– For Staff

We promise to value our ministry of leadership to our congregation as a team and to offer our primary loyalty to that team.

We promise to express criticism and negative feelings first to the person, not to others.

We promise to refuse to talk with a complainer until that person addresses the person she or he is complaining about.

We promise to maintain confidentiality in staff conversations and meetings.

We promise to explain clearly to people who bring staff complaints that we will be sharing the conversation with staff.

We promise to commit to processing information about personality differences among staff and to give feedback to one another in order to support strengths and to balance weaknesses.

We promise to openly discuss our personal strategies and investments in proposals being made.

We promise to accept the fact that disagreements are expected and are to take place behind closed staff doors; in public we present ourselves as a team.